2
K

New California Cuisine

NEW CALIFORNIA

COMPILED AND EDITED BY ROSE DOSTI,
LOS ANGELES TIMES FOOD STAFF

HARRY N. ABRAMS, INC., PUBLISHERS, NEW YORK

CUISINE

Project Director: DARLENE GEIS
Editor: RUTH A. PELTASON
Designer: ANA ROGERS

Library of Congress Cataloging-in-Publication Data

Dosti, Rose.
　　New California cuisine.

　　Includes index.
　　1. Cookery, American — California style.
I. Los Angeles times. II. Title.
TX715.D68754　1986　　641.59794'9　　86–1240
ISBN 0–8109–1293–7

The recipes for Fromage Blanc and Plumped Poussin first appeared in
Chèvre! The Goat Cheese Cookbook, by Laura Chenel and Linda Siegfried,
and are used with the permission of the publisher, Peaks Pike Publish-
ing Co./Aris Books.

The recipe for Grilled Tuna Salad by Ken Frank and Dewey Gram,
© 1984, will appear in a forthcoming book to be published by Simon &
Schuster.

The recipe for Arista is from *Cucina Fresca* by Viana La Place and Evan
Kleiman copyright © 1985 by Viana La Place and Evan Kleiman.
Reprinted by permission of Harper and Row, Publishers, Inc.

The recipe Eggs with Salmon and Sorrel Sauce is from *Modern French
Cooking* by Wolfgang Puck copyright © 1981 by Wolfgang Puck.
Reprinted by permission of Houghton Mifflin Co.

Illustrations copyright © 1986 by *Los Angeles Times*

Times Mirror Books

Printed and bound in Japan

Contents

Introduction   8

Starters   12

Soups   35

Vegetables   44

Salads   60

Pasta, Pizza, Rice, and Eggs   80

Fish and Shellfish   95

Poultry and Game   116

Meat   131

Sweet Things   144

Credits   164

Acknowledgments   165

Index   168

Laura Chenel

Alice Waters and her daughter Fanny

Michel Blanchet

Patrick Terrail

Celestino Drago

Wolfgang Puck

Evan Kleiman

Patrick Jamon

Chef Emilio Nunez and La Scala owner Jean Leon

7

INTRODUCTION

The recipes gathered in this cookbook reflect the culinary revolution that has taken place in California—and especially in Los Angeles—in the last five years. It was a change inspired by the unique and bountiful food supply at hand, the climate, our life-style, the influx of professional chefs from France, Italy, and Japan, and the growing Mexican, Oriental, and Middle Eastern populations on our shores. Certainly the nouvelle cuisine movement in France had its influence on cooking here as elsewhere. These elements have joined in the creation of a trend-setting food style that is being eagerly adopted all over the world. For those who would like to enjoy the new California cuisine at home, we have chosen representative recipes from our great restaurants, chefs, vineyard owners, a few local gastronomes, and some favorites from the files of the *Los Angeles Times*. All have been tested and prepared in the *Times*'s test kitchens.

Perhaps the best way to define California cuisine is in terms of the restaurants and chefs that have helped to create it. There are the pioneers—the solid, established group, who have been part of the California scene ever since Hollywood's heyday and beyond. They set the mood and direction of the restaurant style for those who followed. Culinary individualism began with such early restaurants as Scandia, La Scala, Trader Vic's, The Brown Derby, Musso & Frank Grill, Madame Wu's Garden, The Bistro, and Chasen's in Los Angeles. Further north in the San Francisco area, the Blue Fox, Ernie's, Fournou's Oven, and many others were making their distinctive statements. Two different styles. Both individual.

Social and economic forces of the 1960s and 1970s were responsible for bringing to California professional chefs from Italy and France, and cuisines that dazzled the American palate. Travel abroad had created a more sophisticated patron of dining. The appreciative audience was rewarded by the efforts of such well-trained—and daring—restaurateurs as Patrick Terrail and his chef, Wolfgang Puck, of Ma Maison. Terrail loosened up an otherwise stuffy classical French cuisine by introducing casual chic to the restaurant scene: elegant food served on plastic tables with a full view of celebrities. Puck, his chef, brought new ethnic ideas such as Italian pasta, pizza, and things Chinese, which he eventually incorporated in his own restaurants, Spago and Chinois on Main. Some of these recipes will be found in this book.

Among other French restaurateurs, the late Jean Bertranou and his chef, Michel Blanchet, of L'Ermitage, Paul Bruggemans and the late Camille Bardot of Le St. Germain, Gerard and Virginie Ferry of L'Orangerie, and Bernard Jacoupy of Bernard's, brought Parisian elegance to Los Angeles. For the first time, diners in California could dine on la nouvelle cuisine.

Italian cooking, once associated mainly with pizzerias, suddenly found new expression when Piero Selvaggio of Valentino and Emilio Baglioni of Emilio's began to serve Italian dishes few had ever tasted. They were not dishes with the familiar heavy tomato sauces. They were dishes of Italy's northern regions—delicate white veal piccata, for one. Slightly later came Mauro Vincenti, who created a veritable stage setting in one of the most beautiful restaurants in the world, Rex Il Ristorante, where he presented ultra-refined, modern Italian cooking.

Suddenly, a new school of young chefs entered the scene with novel and exciting ideas. This crop of chefs drew inspiration from the lively mix of cultures, the ethnic markets, and the bountiful land and sea around them. They abstracted ideas of French and Japanese chefs and then combined them. They used their imaginations. They experimented.

Ken Frank, a young American who had some training in French kitchens, opened the first of such innovative restaurants, making use of California-grown and ethnic products, French technique, and original ideas. (He is now at La Toque in Los Angeles.) Michael McCarty, owner of Michael's in Santa Monica, and chef Michael Roberts of Trumps in Los Angeles, are two other pioneers of the new California cuisine. There was Frank using Japanese products to create a French dish. There was Roberts serving potato pancakes and fried pasta to discerning diners. There was McCarty serving baby vegetables so tiny that a single bite finished them off. McCarty became a staunch supporter of small portions. "Beyond ten bites you are a glutton," was his credo. He also encouraged the development of exotic food products, such as the baby vegetables, specially grown ducks, and other commodities for the boutique food industry serving restaurants. Some of the recipes of these trailblazing restaurants are in this book.

If Wolfgang Puck is thought of as the father of the new California cuisine, then Alice Waters must be its mother. At her restaurant, Chez Panisse, in Berkeley, she used fresh local ingredients in a style adapted from French and Italian country cooking. Her style helped crystallize the philosophic base of the new California cuisine. The land and the cuisine became one. It was Waters who lifted pizza from its humdrum existence and gave it culinary importance, using fresh ingredients now found in California—goat cheese, shiitake mushrooms, and the like—because they were more accessible than costly imports. Her recipe for calzone (pizza in turnover form) is included here.

Today there is a new crop of young, energetic innovators who continue to add unusual elements to what has become known as California cuisine. In their hands California cuisine is dynamic, ever-changing, and experimental, as they make use of the increasing variety of foodstuffs that are readily available. The cooking done by these young chefs is highly individual. Roy Yamaguchi of 385 North in Los Angeles epitomizes the new California cuisine chef. He blends his classical French training with American ingenuity and his native Japanese artistry. Duck salad garnished with Japanese dumplings (called gyoza) serves as an example of this innovative mix.

Susan Feniger and Mary Sue Milliken, the vivacious duo from City Café (now Border Grill) and City restaurant find their culinary influence south of the border. They present such bright new dishes as their zingy version of chiles rellenos at Border Grill.

Laurent Quenioux, a classic French chef, uses American ingredients and French techniques with extraordinary skill at his modestly named Seventh Street Bistro. His duck pâté made with a specially developed duck liver, enhances the starters section.

Joachim Splichal, a protégé of the brilliant Jacques Maximin of the Negresco Hotel in Nice, brings originality and a South-of-France flavor to his restaurant, Max au Triangle, with dishes like Small Stuffed Vegetables with Shrimp Ratatouille and Two Sauces.

John Sedlar, a bright star in this stellar group, adds touches from his native American Southwest to French cooking with novel Blue Corn Tortillas with Smoked Salmon and American Caviar.

There are others—many others—such as Susumu Fukui of La Petite Chaya and Chaya Brasserie whose Franco-Japanese inventions are grounded in a virtuoso combination of classical French and gourmet Japanese (*kaiseki*) cooking. His asparagus salad covered with a transparent coat of arrowroot starch is a pure example. The roster grows: Elka Gilmore of Camelions, Patrick Healy of Colette, and Joe Venezia of the Hotel Bel-Air. Some of their recipes and ideas will also be found here.

Further north, a group of chefs in and around San Francisco and Sonoma County paint a dazzling culinary picture with their cooking. Among them Jeremiah Tower of Stars, Narsai David of Narsai's, and John Ash of John Ash & Co. restaurant in Santa Rosa, among many others are distinctive. Some of them, too, have shared recipes.

And there is no end in sight. The cuisine evolves constantly with new ideas and expressions. That's the California way.

ROSE DOSTI

STARTERS

OYSTERS WITH THREE SAUCES
Elka Gilmore, Camelions

TOMMY'S ROLL
Tommy Tang, Tommy Tang's Siamese Café

KUSHIKATSU
Yoriki

SATAY
Victor Sodsook, Siamese Princess Restaurant

AHI CARPACCIO
Michael's

VITELLO MARINATO PARMIGIANO E OLIO DI
    TARTUFO
Rex Il Ristorante

ONION MARMALADE TOAST
Claude Alrivy, Le Chardonnay

DUCK PÂTÉ
Laurent Quenioux, Seventh Street Bistro

HUNTER'S TOAST
(Crostini di Cacciagione)
Mario Quattrucci, Orlando-Orsini Ristorante

GALANTINE WITH CORN AND RED PEPPER
Roy Yamaguchi, 385 North

CHILES RELLENOS
Mary Sue Milliken and Susan Feniger, Border Grill

GREEN CHILES STUFFED WITH MUSHROOM
    DUXELLES
John Sedlar, St. Estèphe

THREE-COLOR TAMALES WITH BELUGA BUTTER
John Sedlar, St. Estèphe

BLUE CORN TORTILLAS WITH SMOKED SALMON AND
    AMERICAN CAVIAR
John Sedlar, St. Estèphe

EGGPLANT SANDWICHES
Claudio Marchesan, Prego

CRISP-FRIED PASTA NIBBLES
Susan Kranwinkle and Peggy Rahn, Inner Gourmet

SAVORY FILO CHEESE CUPS
Gary Danko, Beringer Vineyards

BLACK AND WHITE TORTELLI-ON-A-STICK
Piero Selvaggio, Primi

JUMBO SHELLS AND CHEESE APPETIZERS

PARTY SALSA

PÂTÉ DIANA

SOUTHWESTERN CHICKEN TERRINE

One cannot separate the new California cuisine from its ethnic influences. Culinary exchanges with the large population of Hispanics (5.5 million in California) and the growing Oriental population (2.2 million encompassing Japanese, Chinese, Korean, and Southeast Asian groups) continue to shape our tastes in food. Among the starters (hors d'oeuvres and appetizers) that follow, you will find some delicious examples of this cross-cultural interplay.

At Michael's restaurant, the traditional Italian appetizer of carpaccio undergoes a Japanese sea change when fresh tuna, sliced paper-thin, takes the place of beef. A flourish of shaved truffles tops off this new California marriage of East and West to make Ahi Carpaccio on page 18, a light and flavorful introduction to a meal.

Many of the new dishes that delight the palate are based upon products launched in Sonoma County's recently established boutique food industries. Jack and cheddar cheeses have been made there for some years. More recently Laura Chenel started the first goat cheese industry in the United States. Her cheeses have inspired creative chefs such as Alice Waters of Chez Panisse, whose signature warm goat cheese salad has swept the country. At Beringer Vineyards, Gary Danko makes a goat cheese hors d'oeuvre, Savory Filo Cheese Cups, page 28, combining Greek pastry and two kinds of goat cheese in a tender and flavorful tidbit to tempt the appetite.

OYSTERS WITH THREE SAUCES
Elka Gilmore, Camelions

24 oysters, on the half shell
Basil-Red Pepper Sauce (recipe follows)
Citrus-Ginger Sauce (recipe follows)
Mignonette Sauce (recipe follows)

Place the oysters on a napkin-lined tray or platter. Surround them with 3 bowls containing the basil-red pepper sauce, citrus-ginger sauce, and mignonette sauce. Allow guests to ladle desired sauce over oysters.

MAKES 6 SERVINGS

Basil-Red Pepper Sauce

1 bunch basil, finely shredded
1 large red pepper, peeled, seeded, and cut into fine
  julienne strips
½ cup rice wine vinegar
Juice of 2 lemons
1 clove garlic, minced
Salt
Cracked black pepper

Combine the basil, red pepper, vinegar, lemon juice, garlic, and salt and pepper to taste. Mix well.

MAKES ABOUT 1 CUP

Citrus-Ginger Sauce

Juice of 1 orange
Juice of 1 lemon
Juice of 1 lime
1 teaspoon minced ginger root
1 drop sesame oil
Pinch cayenne pepper
Chopped fresh mint, for garnish

Combine the orange, lemon, and lime juices in a bowl. Stir in the ginger root, sesame oil, and cayenne. Mix well. Garnish with mint.

MAKES ABOUT ¾ CUP

Mignonette Sauce

1 cup raspberry vinegar
20 peppercorns, cracked
3 shallots, peeled and minced

Combine the raspberry vinegar, peppercorns, and shallots. Let stand to blend flavors.

MAKES ABOUT 1 CUP

TOMMY'S ROLL
Tommy Tang, Tommy Tang's Siamese Café

1 large package freshwater eel, about 6 to 8 ounces
Sweet Rice (recipe page 16)
8 (8-inch) seaweed squares, cut in halves
¼ pound smoked salmon, cut into thin strips
Sweet Eggs (recipe page 16)
Packaged radish sprouts
Black sesame seeds
White sesame seeds
½ cup soy sauce
1 teaspoon prepared Japanese horseradish

Cut the eel into pieces 3 inches long and ¼-inch wide. Place the strips in a toaster oven and heat for 10 minutes. Set aside.

Spread the sweet rice on the entire surface of each seaweed sheet half, pressing rice to adhere to seaweed. Fold the rice-lined sheet to resemble a cone shape. Fill each cone with strips of eel, salmon, sweet eggs, and radish sprouts. Sprinkle with black and white sesame seeds.

Mix soy sauce with Japanese horseradish in a small bowl and serve as a dip.

MAKES 16 CONES

Note: Packaged eel comes in small, medium, and large vacuum packages. All ingredients are available at most Japanese food stores.

Assorted cheeses

Sweet Rice

1 cup Japanese-style rice
1 cup water
2 tablespoons sugar
¼ teaspoon salt
2 tablespoons sake
Dash soy sauce

Place the rice and water in an automatic rice cooker and cook as directed by manufacturer, until rice is tender. Transfer rice to a bowl, and add the sugar, salt, sake, and soy sauce. Mix well.

MAKES 2 CUPS RICE

Note: If an automatic rice cooker is unavailable, cook rice 5 to 7 minutes longer than suggested on rice package, or until rice is very soft and sticky.

Sweet Eggs

2 eggs
1 tablespoon sake
1 tablespoon water
1 tablespoon sugar
Pinch salt
1 tablespoon oil or butter

Beat the eggs with sake, water, sugar, and salt in a bowl. Heat the oil or melt the butter in a 6-inch skillet. Pour egg mixture into skillet. Cook as for an omelet, and fold in half. Turn out of skillet, and cut into ½-inch strips, or enough to make 16 strips.

KUSHIKATSU
Yoriki

6 eggs
1 cup milk
1 cup flour, sifted
½ teaspoon sugar
1 small Japanese cup sake (about 1 ounce)
Any tender meat, fish, shellfish, poultry, or fresh vegetables cut into bite-size pieces or cubes (see list, page 17)
Bread crumbs or chopped almonds

Soy oil for deep frying
Tonkatsu Sauce (recipe follows)
Miso Dip for vegetables (recipe follows)

Beat the eggs, then beat in the milk, flour, sugar, and sake until smooth. Thread bite-size pieces of meat, fish, shellfish, poultry, or fresh vegetables on long bamboo skewers. Dip skewered food into the batter, then roll in bread crumbs. Skewers may be refrigerated at this point.

When ready to cook, heat the oil to 360 degrees in a deep-fat fryer fitted with a basket. Add the skewers to the hot oil, a few at a time to prevent crowding, and cook quickly, depending on the food. Drain on paper towels. Continue to fry remaining skewers.

Serve kushikatsu while hot on a tray with small amounts of tonkatsu sauce and miso dip.

ENOUGH BATTER FOR ABOUT 50 KUSHIKATSU

Note: If you want to serve all of the kushikatsu together, you may keep the just-cooked ones in a warm oven.

Tonkatsu Sauce

2 cups bottled tonkatsu sauce
2 cups chicken broth
1 tablespoon curry powder

Combine tonkatsu sauce, chicken broth, and curry powder in a blender. Blend until smooth. Pour into a saucepan and simmer over very low heat for 1½ hours. Cool, then refrigerate to use as needed.

MAKES ABOUT 4 CUPS

Note: Bottled tonkatsu sauce is available at Japanese grocery stores.

Miso Dip

½ cup white miso
¾ cup sake
½ cup mirin (rice wine)
1 to 2 tablespoons sugar
1 tablespoon tahini (sesame seed paste)

Combine the miso, sake, mirin, sugar, and tahini in a saucepan. Bring to a boil. Reduce heat and simmer over medium-low heat for 10 minutes, stirring often. Cool before serving.

MAKES ABOUT 1¾ CUPS

Note: White miso fermented rice and soybean paste is available at any Oriental grocery store.

SUGGESTED FOODS FOR KUSHIKATSU

Clams—Dip each clam in batter, roll in crushed almonds, and then in bread crumbs.

Crab legs or slices with seaweed—Season crab with salt and white pepper. Cut a square of seaweed large enough to wrap around crab. Place the crab in the center of a square. Wrap seaweed around the crab. Skewer with double-pronged skewer, if available.

Cheese—Any cheese may be used. For medium cheddar, cut into ½-inch cubes. Place each cube on a small won ton skin. Fold the won ton sheet, moistening seams to secure.

Stuffed peppers—Season ground sirloin with salt, pepper, and finely chopped green onions. Shape the meat into a small ball. Remove the seeds and membranes of bell peppers. Cut into squares. Place some meat in center of skewer. Anchor with squares of green pepper.

Chicken livers—Cook the chicken livers in water to cover with sake, soy sauce, and fresh ginger in a saucepan for about 10 minutes or until chicken livers are done. Reserve cooking liquid. Cut livers in half. Sandwich 2 pieces of liver between slices of fresh ginger. Marinate overnight in cooking liquid.

Chinese pea pods—Trim off ends, and thread lengthwise on skewers.

Steak—Season rib eye steak with salt and pepper. Cut into ½-inch cubes.

Tofu—Cut into ½-inch cubes. Place on the end of the skewer.

Scallops—Season with salt, pepper, and soy sauce.

Shrimp—Season with salt, pepper, and soy sauce.

Chicken with celery—Sandwich small cubes of chicken breast fillet between celery slices.

Potato and bacon—Parboil potato; do not overcook or the potato will fall apart. Cut into ½-inch cubes. Sandwich cubes of potato between 2 (1-inch) squares of bacon.

SATAY
Victor Sodsook, Siamese Princess Restaurant

1 pound long, flat slices of chicken breast, lean pork, beef, or lamb
3 cloves garlic, minced
½ onion, minced
2 teaspoons minced cilantro
1 tablespoon brown sugar
Juice of 1 lime
1 tablespoon fish sauce
1 tablespoon vegetable oil
Peanut Butter Sauce (recipe follows)

Thread the meat on 12-inch bamboo skewers, placing several strips on each of 16 skewers. Combine the garlic, onion, cilantro, brown sugar, lime juice, fish sauce, and vegetable oil in a bowl. Pour over the skewers and marinate for 1 hour.

Heat barbecue coals until hot, or preheat a broiler. Place the skewers on the grill or broiler rack and cook until done as desired. Serve the satays with peanut butter sauce.

MAKES 16 SKEWERS, ENOUGH FOR 16 APPETIZERS

Peanut Butter Sauce

½ cup crunchy peanut butter
1 onion, minced
1 stalk lemon grass, minced
1 cup coconut milk
1 tablespoon brown sugar
1 teaspoon chile powder
1 tablespoon fish sauce
1 tablespoon heavy soy sauce

Combine the peanut butter, onion, lemon grass, coconut milk, brown sugar, chile powder, fish sauce, and soy sauce in a saucepan. Bring the sauce to a boil. Remove from the heat, and pour into small bowls to serve.

MAKES ABOUT 1½ CUPS

AHI CARPACCIO
Michael's

½ pound fresh tuna, sliced paper-thin
Salt
Oil
Vinegar
Freshly cracked pepper
1 bunch arugula
Grated Parmesan cheese
½ to 1 white or black fresh (or canned) truffle, shaved

Arrange the tuna in overlapping slices on a platter. Sprinkle with salt and drizzle with oil and vinegar to taste. Sprinkle with pepper. Surround the tuna with a wreath of arugula. Sprinkle grated Parmesan cheese over all. Top with truffle shavings.

MAKES 4 APPETIZER SERVINGS

VITELLO MARINATO PARMIGIANO E OLIO DI TARTUFO
Rex Il Ristorante

8 paper-thin slices sirloin of veal
Truffle Sauce (recipe follows)
2 small heads radicchio
8 paper-thin slices Parmesan cheese
Celery leaves, for garnish

Dip each veal slice in the truffle sauce, and chill for at least 1 hour. When ready to serve, shred the radicchio and mix with ¼ cup of the truffle sauce. Place equal portions of radicchio on 4 salad plates. Arrange 2 slices marinated veal and 2 slices Parmesan cheese on top. Garnish with celery leaves.

MAKES 4 SERVINGS

Note: If radicchio is unavailable, use any firm-type lettuce, such as endive or iceberg lettuce. To cut Parmesan cheese into paper-thin slices, try using a potato peeler.

Truffle Sauce

1 egg yolk
½ cup olive oil

Juice of ½ lemon
Salt, pepper
Few drops truffle oil or walnut oil

Beat the egg yolk in a small bowl. Gradually add olive oil and beat until slightly thickened. Blend in the lemon juice and season to taste with salt and pepper. Stir in truffle oil.

Note: Any nut-flavored oil may be used in place of truffle oil.

ONION MARMALADE TOAST
Claude Alrivy, Le Chardonnay

24 French bread slices, cut ½-inch thick
Butter, softened
Onion Marmalade (recipe follows)
12 quail eggs, cooked
24 large watercress leaves

Spread both sides of each bread slice with butter. Toast both sides until golden. Spread with the onion marmalade. Garnish each slice of toast with half a quail egg and a watercress leaf.

MAKES 24 APPETIZERS

Onion Marmalade

¼ cup butter
2½ to 3 cups minced onions
½ cup red wine vinegar
1 cup red wine
5½ tablespoons sugar
2 teaspoons salt
1 teaspoon white pepper
¼ cup grenadine syrup

Melt the butter in a sauté pan. Add the onions and sauté until tender, but not brown. Add the wine vinegar, red wine, sugar, salt, and pepper. Simmer for 5 minutes. Add the grenadine. Cook until reduced to a thick marmalade consistency, about 45 minutes. Add more wine or water if necessary to keep marmalade from scorching.

MAKES ABOUT 1 CUP MARMALADE

Laurent Quenioux with Duck Pâté (page 20)

DUCK PÂTÉ
Laurent Quenioux, Seventh Street Bistro

1 (1½-pound) mallard liver
1 cup good quality port
1 cup Cognac
1½ to 2 teaspoons salt
½ teaspoon white pepper
Truffle slices, optional
Endive leaves, optional
Crackers, optional

Separate the lobes of the liver. Slit lobes to remove the large vein attached to the 2 large and 1 small liver lobes. Press small lobe through strainer to purée, and set aside.

Place large lobes in shallow pan. Pour port and Cognac over livers. Sprinkle with salt to taste and pepper on both sides. Marinate 30 to 40 minutes, turning every 10 minutes.

Butterfly large lobes and press them into a 6-inch terrine, filling any air spaces with the strained liver. Pack firmly. Place terrine in larger pan filled halfway with water. Bake at 200 degrees for 45 minutes. Fat will rise to surface. Do not remove. Cool.

Cut cardboard to size of terrine opening, cover with foil, and press firmly onto foie gras to weight it down. Pour off excess fat, leaving a thin layer in pan. Weight down with a brick, or similar heavy object. Refrigerate 2 to 3 hours.

To serve, cut foie gras with a warm knife into ¼-inch slices. Place on serving plate. Decorate center with truffle slices, endive leaves, or other greens, if desired. Or serve at end of meal allowing guests to scoop out foie gras to spread over crackers.

MAKES ENOUGH FOIE GRAS FOR 10 TO 12 SERVINGS

Note: Serve with sweet, perfumy wine such as Château Yquem or a sauvignon blanc.

Variation: Duck Pâté with Chanterelles or Asparagus
For a layered pâté, divide the duck liver into thirds. Poach about ½ pound chanterelle mushrooms or asparagus spears in a small amount of chicken stock until tender. Place a layer of the mushroom caps or asparagus spears over one layer of liver pressed into the terrine. Top with more liver. Cover with another layer of mushroom caps. Top with a final liver layer. Bake as directed.

HUNTER'S TOAST
(Crostini di Cacciagione)
Mario Quattrucci, Orlando-Orsini Ristorante

1 bunch fresh rosemary
1 small bunch fresh sage
1 bunch parsley, chopped
A few basil leaves
3 bay leaves
6 juniper berries
2 to 3 cloves garlic
½ medium onion, peeled and chopped
1 ounce chicken livers
2 whole boneless wild duck breasts, chopped
1 whole boneless breast of wild pheasant, chopped
1 anchovy fillet, chopped
2 tablespoons capers
Oil
1 ounce brandy
3 ounces gin
2 French rolls, cut up
Bread rolls, sliced ¼-inch-thick, toasted
Parsley, for garnish

In a large bowl combine the rosemary, sage, parsley, basil, bay leaves, juniper berries, garlic, onion, chicken livers, duck and pheasant breasts, anchovy, and capers.

Heat 2 tablespoons oil in a large skillet. Add the herb-and-game mixture, and sauté until the duck and pheasant are golden brown. Add the brandy and gin; cook until the liquid evaporates. Remove from heat, and discard bay leaves.

Place the mixture in a food processor fitted with the steel blade. Add the French rolls and process until a smooth pâté is formed. Gradually add 2 cups oil. Process until well blended. Chill.

To serve, spread on sliced toasted bread or mound the pâté on a platter lined with the toast. Garnish with parsley.

MAKES 20 SERVINGS

GALANTINE WITH CORN AND RED PEPPER
Roy Yamaguchi, 385 North

1 (3- to 3½-pound) chicken
2 tablespoons madeira
Salt, pepper
1 (¾-pound) pork butt
Panada (recipe follows)
¼ cup olive oil
2 small red peppers, diced
2 small green peppers, diced
10 mushrooms, diced
1 ear corn, kernels removed and chopped
1 cup chicken stock, approximately
Orange-Chile Mayonnaise (recipe follows)

Remove the chicken wings at the second joint. Split the skin from the chicken neck to tail along the spine; refrigerate to solidify the fat.

Bone the chicken, starting at skin openings in the back and working toward the breast. Reserve the skin. Remove breast meat and cut into ½-inch cubes. Place the breast meat in a bowl and add madeira and salt and pepper to taste. Set aside. Grind the remaining chicken meat and pork butt in a food processor. Add the panada to the chicken-pork mixture.

Heat the olive oil in a skillet. Sauté the red and green peppers, mushrooms, and corn kernels until the peppers are tender. Cool, then add to the panada and meat mixture. Lay the chicken skin on a piece of cheesecloth, skin side down. Over it spread the mixture to within 1 inch of the edges. Drain the cubed chicken breast, then place over the galantine mixture. Roll, jelly-roll fashion, using the cheesecloth for leverage.

Wrap the roll in more cheesecloth, twisting ends tightly to form a compact roll. Tie the ends with twine. Place the roll in a roasting pan and add the chicken stock. Cover, and simmer for about 1 hour, or 25 minutes per pound, until done. Add more stock if needed. Remove from pan and cool at room temperature. Chill overnight. When ready to serve, remove the cheesecloth and slice the galantine. Serve with the orange-chile mayonnaise.

MAKES ABOUT 12 SERVINGS

Panada

2 eggs
1 teaspoon salt
½ teaspoon French four-spice
½ teaspoon brandy
¾ cup flour
½ cup half and half

Beat the eggs, salt, four-spice, and brandy, blending well. Whisk in the flour until smooth. Gradually add half and half until the panada is the consistency of thick cream.

Orange-Chile Mayonnaise

1 cup orange juice
2 egg yolks
1 tablespoon Dijon mustard
1 tablespoon grated ginger
1 teaspoon chopped cilantro
2 jalapeño chiles, minced
1 cup olive oil
Dash vinegar, optional

Boil the orange juice in a saucepan until reduced to a syrupy consistency. Remove from heat and cool. Whisk in the egg yolks, mustard, ginger, cilantro, and chiles. Gradually whisk or use blender to add the oil until mixture forms a mayonnaise. Add vinegar. Thin with additional orange juice if too thick.

MAKES ABOUT 2 CUPS

CHILES RELLENOS
Mary Sue Milliken and Susan Feniger, Border Grill

6 poblano chiles
1 cup grated Mexican cheese, such as añejo
½ cup crumbled fresh Mexican cheese, such as queso fresco (pot cheese or farmer cheese may be substituted)
1 cup flour
3 eggs, beaten
¼ cup butter
Red Salsa (recipe page 24)
Green Salsa (recipe page 24)
Sour cream

TOP: *John Sedlar*

BOTTOM: *Three-Color Tamales with Beluga Butter (page 25)*

RIGHT: *A St. Estèphe southwestern spread, from the left—Blue Corn Tortillas with Smoked Salmon and American Caviar (page 28); Terrine of Salmon, Corn, and Jalapeños (page 97); Green Chiles Stuffed with Mushroom Duxelles (page 24); and platter of tamales*

Roast the chiles either under the broiler or over a gas burner on all sides until charred, but not burned. Place immediately in a plastic bag to steam until cooled. Then carefully peel the chiles. Slit along one side (do not cut in half) and remove the seeds. Rinse under cool water to remove excess skin or seeds.

Toss the cheeses together and press into 6 oblong shapes large enough to fit into the chiles. Wrap each chile around the cheese, being careful that the seams are closed. Dredge each stuffed chile in flour, dusting off any excess.

Dip floured chiles into the beaten eggs. Melt the butter and heat until hot but not browned. Add the chiles, one at a time. Lightly brown on both sides. Serve on bed of red and green salsas with a dollop of sour cream.

MAKES 6 SERVINGS

Red Salsa

2 serrano chiles, stems removed
5 tomatoes, cored and cut into quarters
2 cloves garlic
1 tablespoon butter
1 onion, sliced
Salt to taste

Combine the chiles, tomatoes, and garlic in a blender. Melt the butter, add the onion, and sauté until tender. Add to tomato mixture. Blend until smooth. Strain mixture into a saucepan. Bring to a boil and add salt. Remove from heat; cool. Refrigerate until ready to use. Store any remaining sauce in the refrigerator up to 1 week or in the freezer for up to 6 months.

MAKES ABOUT 1 QUART

Green Salsa

5 or 6 tomatillos
1 tablespoon butter
1 onion, chopped
2 cloves garlic, peeled and halved
1 bunch cilantro
2 cups water
Salt to taste

Remove the core from the tomatillos and cut into quarters. Melt the butter in a small skillet and add the onion. Sauté until the onion is tender.

Place the tomatillos, garlic, cilantro, onion mixture, and water in blender and purée. Strain into a saucepan. Bring to a boil, and add salt to taste. Remove from heat; cool. Store any remaining sauce in refrigerator up to 1 week or in the freezer for up to 6 months.

MAKES ABOUT 3¼ CUPS

GREEN CHILES STUFFED WITH MUSHROOM DUXELLES
John Sedlar, St. Estèphe

¾ pound mushrooms, roughly chopped
½ cup heavy cream
Salt, white pepper
6 poblano chiles or small green peppers, roasted, peeled, and seeded
Crème de Chèvre (recipe follows)

Purée the mushrooms in a food processor. Add the cream and process again. Season to taste with salt and pepper. Make a slit lengthwise in the chiles, remove the seeds, and stuff with the mushroom mixture. Close chiles, wrap in plastic wrap, and steam on a rack set over simmering water for 5 minutes. Serve with crème de chèvre or cover the bottom of a large serving platter with the sauce. Arrange the chiles over the sauce. Serve the chiles with some of the sauce spooned over them.

MAKES 6 SERVINGS

Crème de Chèvre

1 cup heavy cream
2½ ounces goat cheese
½ teaspoon chopped garlic

Bring the cream to a simmer in a saucepan. Add the cheese and garlic. Pass the sauce through a strainer or colander.

MAKES 1⅓ CUPS

THREE-COLOR TAMALES WITH BELUGA BUTTER
John Sedlar, St. Estèphe

6 dried corn husks
About 10 ounces prepared masa
Spinach Mousse (recipe follows)
Scallop Mousse (recipe follows)
Salmon Mousse (recipe follows)
Salmon caviar, approximately 1 ounce
Beluga Butter (recipe follows)
1 cup corn kernels

Soak corn husks in warm water until softened, about 20 minutes. Remove husks and pat dry. Cut them into 4 x 2-inch-wide strips. Knot each corn strip about ¹/₂ inch from the end. Set aside.

Cut eighteen 6-inch square pieces of plastic wrap. On each plastic square place 1 heaping tablespoon prepared masa. Flatten masa into a 1 x 2-inch rectangle. At one end of the masa place 1 scant tablespoon spinach mousse, followed by 1 scant tablespoon salmon mousse, and 1 scant tablespoon scallop mousse. Gently pat into a small loaf, making sure not to mix the mousses (each should be an individual stripe). Place ¹/₄ teaspoon salmon caviar on top of each tamale and tightly enclose with the plastic wrap. Place wrapped tamales on a steamer rack over simmering water. Steam tamales for 5 minutes or until firm.

Place 1 corn husk strip in the center of each plate and spoon about 1 tablespoon beluga butter in the middle of each corn husk. Unwrap tamales and place over the butter. Sprinkle about 1 tablespoon corn kernels around each tamale; serve hot.

MAKES 18 TAMALE APPETIZERS

Note: Prepared masa is available at many meat counters of major supermarkets or at Mexican grocery stores.

Spinach Mousse

1 pound spinach, steamed
1 egg white
3 tablespoons heavy cream
¹/₈ teaspoon salt
¹/₈ teaspoon white pepper

Blend the spinach, egg white, cream, salt, and pepper in a food processor. Process until smooth.

Scallop Mousse

5 ounces scallops
1 egg white
3 tablespoons heavy cream
¹/₈ teaspoon salt
¹/₈ teaspoon white pepper

Blend the scallops, egg white, cream, salt, and pepper in a food processor. Process until smooth.

Salmon Mousse

5 ounces salmon, skinned, boned, and cleaned
1 egg white
3 tablespoons heavy cream
¹/₈ teaspoon salt
¹/₈ teaspoon white pepper

Blend the salmon, egg white, cream, salt, and pepper in a food processor. Process until smooth.

Beluga Butter

1 cup white wine
1 cup white wine vinegar
¹/₂ teaspoon salt
1 tablespoon shallots, minced
1 cup heavy cream
1¹/₃ ounces beluga caviar

Combine the wine, vinegar, salt, and shallots in a large saucepan. Add the cream and reduce by two-thirds. Strain and keep warm. Before using, stir in the caviar.

MAKES ABOUT 1 CUP SAUCE

TOP: *Preparing Satay from the Siamese Princess—chef Victor Sodsook, Pachara and Prapai Suchoknand*

BOTTOM, LEFT: *Elka Gilmore (wearing cap)*

BOTTOM, RIGHT: *Claudio Marchesan*

OPPOSITE: *California shellfish*

Blue Corn Tortillas with Smoked Salmon and American Caviar
John Sedlar, St. Estèphe

8 blue or white corn tortillas
¾ cup creme fraîche or sour cream
½ cup chopped white onion
2 ounces golden or red caviar
2 ounces Tennessee River caviar or other black caviar
2 ounces sliced smoked salmon
20 to 30 capers, for garnish
Fresh dill, for garnish

Slice the tortillas into 24 shapes such as rounds, squares, or triangles. Place on a baking sheet and bake at 350 degrees for 5 to 7 minutes or until heated through.

Divide the tortillas into 3 sets. Place a dollop of crème fraîche and chopped onion on all of them. Then on one set place some golden caviar. Add black caviar to the second set, and sliced salmon on last group. Garnish all the tortillas with capers and dill.

MAKES 24 APPETIZERS

Eggplant Sandwiches
Claudio Marchesan, Prego

1 small eggplant, sliced ¼-inch thick
Coarse salt
Pepper
1 tablespoon chopped fresh basil
1 tablespoon chopped fresh parsley
1 clove garlic, minced
Red wine vinegar
1 teaspoon mashed sun-dried tomato
1 cup fresh goat cheese (Montrachet style)
Chopped parsley, for garnish

Prepare a medium charcoal grill. Place the eggplant slices on a large tray or baking sheet and sprinkle with coarse salt. Let stand to release moisture, about 20 minutes. Drain, rinse, and pat dry.

Sprinkle the eggplant slices on both sides with pepper, basil, parsley, and garlic. Grill over medium coals until wilted but not overcooked, sprinkling with vinegar while cooking. Remove from grill.

Blend the sun-dried tomato into the goat cheese. Spread some on each eggplant slice. Roll, jelly-roll fashion. Arrange the eggplant on a serving tray or platter. Garnish with chopped parsley.

MAKES ABOUT 12 ROLLS

Crisp-Fried Pasta Nibbles
Susan Kranwinkle and Peggy Rahn, Inner Gourmet

Pasta, in desired shapes
Oil for deep frying
Garlic or other seasoned salt

Cook pasta in boiling salted water until almost tender. Drain and pat dry on absorbent towels. Heat oil in a deep sauté pan or heavy skillet to 375 degrees. Add pasta, a few pieces at a time, to the hot oil and cook until lightly browned and crisp. Drain on paper towels and sprinkle with garlic salt. Cool and store in an airtight container.

12 APPETIZER SERVINGS PER POUND OF PASTA

Savory Filo Cheese Cups
Gary Danko, Beringer Vineyards

6 sheets filo pastry
¼ cup hazelnut oil, warmed
Fromage Blanc Filling (recipe follows)
Vegetable oil

Brush each filo pastry sheet with warmed oil and stack sheets. Trim stack to measure 15 x 12 inches. Cut into twenty 3-inch squares. Brush a small cupcake tin with oil. Press each square of dough into a cup. Flatten corners onto the pan to form petals. Chill.

Pour fromage blanc filling into formed cups. Bake at 350 degrees until cups are golden and mixture is lightly puffed.

MAKES 20 CHEESE CUPS

Fromage Blanc Filling

8 ounces fromage blanc (a fresh, soft goat cheese, lightly
  whipped) or cream cheese
2 ounces medium-strong goat cheese, such as Montrachet
  or feta
2 eggs
1/4 cup heavy cream
Salt, pepper
2 medium basil leaves, minced
1/4 teaspoon dried rosemary
1/8 teaspoon dried thyme
1 tablespoon hazelnut oil

Combine the fromage blanc, goat cheese, eggs, cream, salt
and pepper to taste, basil, rosemary, thyme, and oil. Mix
until well blended.

BLACK AND WHITE TORTELLI-ON-A-STICK

Piero Selvaggio, Primi

60 *Black Tortelli* (recipe follows)
60 *White Tortelli* (recipe follows)
Butter, softened
Tomato-Red Pepper Sauce (recipe page 30)
Cream Sauce (recipe page 32)

Cook the tortelli in boiling salted water until they rise to surface, or until tender, about 4 to 5 minutes. (You will need to
cook them in several batches.) Melt about 6 tablespoons butter in a large skillet. Add some of the tortelli and toss to coat
well; remove from pan. Repeat process, adding more butter
if necessary. Thread the tortelli on skewers, allowing 1 black
and white tortelli per skewer. Serve with the tomato-red pepper sauce and cream sauce for dipping.

MAKES 60 APPETIZERS

Note: Store-bought tortelli may be used. Cook and assemble as directed.

Black Tortelli

2 cups flour
2 eggs
1/2 teaspoon oil
1/4 cup water
1/2 teaspoon cuttlefish or squid ink
Seafood Filling (recipe page 30)

Mound the flour on a clean surface. Make a well in the center
of the dough. Add the eggs and oil; blend. Then add the
water and ink and blend in well. Using a fork work the walls
of the flour into the ingredients, mixing to blend until all
the dough is incorporated with liquid ingredients and is
sticky. Knead on a floured board until the dough is smooth
and elastic. Cover and let stand at room temperature, about
30 minutes.

Cut dough into 6 portions. Roll out each portion so that it
will fit into a pasta machine. Feed the pasta through the
machine, starting with the widest setting and progressing to
the finest setting until the pasta is thin (expansion takes
place during cooking). Continue until all the dough is rolled
into strips.

Place each portion on a floured board and lightly flour. Cut
into ten 2-inch squares for miniature tortelli. Let rest 10 minutes before filling and cooking. Place 1 teaspoon seafood filling in the center of each tortelli square. Fold the square into a
triangle, then fold in half lengthwise. Twist the pasta around
your index finger and pinch the corners to seal. Brush edges
with water to seal. Continue cutting other strips until all are
used.

MAKES 60 SMALL TORTELLI

White Tortelli

Repeat procedure for Black Tortelli but omit cuttlefish
ink.

MAKES 60 SMALL TORTELLI

Seafood Filling

1 tablespoon olive oil
2 shallots, chopped
1 clove garlic, minced
¹/₂ pound scallops, chopped
¹/₂ pound shelled shrimp, deveined, cleaned, and chopped
¹/₂ pound sea bass fillets, chopped
¹/₂ cup plus 2 tablespoons dry white wine
1 tablespoon chopped fresh parsley
2 teaspoons chopped fresh basil
Salt, pepper
1 egg

Heat the oil in a skillet. Add the shallots and garlic and cook until lightly browned. Add the scallops, shrimp, sea bass, and wine. Simmer 5 minutes over medium heat. Cool and drain any excess liquid, then add the parsley, basil, and salt and pepper to taste. Stir in the egg, mixing well.

MAKES ABOUT 4 CUPS

Tomato-Red Pepper Sauce

2 tablespoons olive oil
1 clove garlic, minced
1 cup chopped tomato
¹/₂ sweet red pepper, finely diced
¹/₄ cup chardonnay
1 teaspoon chopped fresh basil
1 tablespoon heavy cream, approximately
Salt

Heat the oil in a skillet. Add the garlic and sauté until golden. Add tomato and red pepper. Sauté until the red pepper is tender. Add the chardonnay and cook until slightly reduced, about 3 minutes. Stir in the basil. Pour into a blender and blend until smooth. If too thick, add the cream to make a consistency for dipping. Add salt to taste.

MAKES ABOUT 1 CUP

ABOVE, RIGHT: *Piero Selvaggio displaying Black and White Tortelli-on-a-Stick (page 29)*

OPPOSITE: *Pâté Diana (page 32) and Walnut Bread (page 156)*

Cream Sauce

1 cup fish stock
1 cup chardonnay
6 tablespoons unsalted butter
2 teaspoons chopped chives
Salt, pepper
½ cup heavy cream

Simmer the stock until reduced by half. Add the chardonnay and simmer until slightly reduced. Add butter, stirring until blended in. Add chives, and salt and pepper to taste. Add the cream and simmer for 10 minutes or until bubbly and thickened.

MAKES ABOUT 1 CUP

Jumbo Shells and Cheese Appetizers

12 jumbo pasta shells
Oil for deep frying
2 tablespoons grated Parmesan cheese
¼ teaspoon chili powder
1½ cups cheddar cheese
2 cloves garlic, pressed
1 tablespoon chopped parsley
¼ cup sour cream
¼ cup chopped black olives

Cook the pasta shells in a large pot of boiling salted water for 12 minutes. Drain well — let stand at least 30 minutes until completely drained. In a deep skillet heat oil to 400 degrees. Fry the shells 1 to 1½ minutes until crisp. Drain on paper towels. The shells may be prepared in advance and stored in a covered container.

Roll the shells in Parmesan cheese mixed with chili powder. Combine the cheddar cheese, garlic, parsley, sour cream, and olives. Stuff the shells with this mixture. Serve as is or bake just enough to heat through. To heat, prop the shells in foil to stand upright on baking tray. Bake at 400 degrees for 8 to 10 minutes until cheese is melted.

MAKES 12 APPETIZERS

Party Salsa

4 large, firm tomatoes, chopped
3 tomatillos, finely chopped
1 medium onion, finely chopped
3 green onions, thinly sliced
½ green pepper, chopped
1 green jalapeño chile, finely chopped
2 yellow chiles, finely chopped
3 tablespoons chopped cilantro
1 teaspoon minced garlic
4 drops hot pepper sauce
2 tablespoons red wine vinegar
Salt

In a large bowl, combine the tomatoes, tomatillos, onion, green onions, green pepper, jalapeño chile, yellow chiles, cilantro, garlic, hot pepper sauce, and vinegar. Blend well and season to taste with salt.

MAKES 7 CUPS

Pâté Diana

1 cup butter
½ cup chopped onions
2 tablespoons chopped shallots
¼ cup chopped, peeled apples
1 pound chicken livers, cut in halves
¼ cup apple wine or brandy
2 to 3 tablespoons heavy cream
1 teaspoon lemon juice
1 teaspoon salt
¼ teaspoon black pepper
½ cup clarified butter (see note)
Apple slices for garnish, optional

Soften 10 tablespoons of the butter and set aside. Melt 3 tablespoons butter in a skillet. Add the onions and shallots. Cook until tender, stirring, about 5 minutes. Add the apples and cook until tender, about 3 minutes. Place the apple mixture in a blender.

Melt another 3 tablespoons butter in the skillet. Add the chicken livers and stir 3 to 4 minutes until the livers are browned outside and pink inside. Add the wine and stir 2 minutes longer. Add the liver mixture to the blender. Add 2 tablespoons cream and blend at high speed until smooth.

Add more cream, if necessary, to make the mixture smooth. Press through a medium-fine strainer into a mixing bowl. Cool thoroughly, stirring once or twice. (The pâté will become oily if not completely cooled.)

In another bowl, cream the softened 10 tablespoons butter with an electric mixer and add the liver mixture, a little at a time, beating well after each addition. Stir in the lemon juice, salt, and pepper. Pour the pâté into a crock or ramekins, smoothing the top with a spatula. Pour enough clarified butter over the top to form a seal. Serve chilled and garnished with apple slices, if desired. Store in refrigerator up to 1 week or freeze, in appropriate containers, if desired. Serve with sliced and lightly toasted Rancho Bernardo Inn's Walnut Bread (page 156).

MAKES 8 TO 12 SERVINGS

Note: To clarify butter, cut butter into small pieces and melt it over low heat. Once melted, skim off the foam that has collected on the surface, and carefully draw off the resulting golden butter, leaving behind the milky residue that has collected in the bottom of the saucepan.

The recipe for the pâté may be doubled, if desired.

SOUTHWESTERN CHICKEN TERRINE

2 tablespoons chopped shallots
2 tablespoons butter or margarine
3/4 pound chicken breasts, boned, skinned, and cubed
1/2 cup oil
1/4 cup chicken broth
1 1/2 teaspoons chopped fresh oregano
2 eggs
Salt
Freshly ground black pepper
3/4 pound chicken thighs, boned, skinned, and cubed
1 (4-ounce) can whole green chiles, sliced in half
  lengthwise, seeds removed
1 cup pitted black olives, halved lengthwise
1/2 cup corn kernels
2 or 3 green onions
4 or 5 carrot slices
Cilantro Sauce (recipe follows)

Sauté shallots in butter until soft. In a food processor combine the chicken breast meat with half of the shallots and half amounts *each* of the oil, chicken broth, and oregano. Add 1 egg. Season to taste with salt and pepper. Process until smooth. Transfer mixture to a bowl and set aside.

Place the thigh meat in the processor and add remaining shallots, oil, broth, oregano, and egg. Season to taste with salt and pepper. Process until smooth. Transfer to a bowl and set aside.

Place half of the chicken breast mixture in a buttered terrine or an 8 x 4-inch loaf pan. Cover with a layer of green chiles, arranged lengthwise. Add remaining chicken breast mixture, spreading to form an even layer. Arrange a single layer of olives, lengthwise, over the chicken, pressing the olives lightly into the chicken. Next add half of the chicken thigh mixture, spreading evenly. Cover with a layer of corn, spreading evenly. Add remaining chicken thigh mixture and spread evenly. Cover with buttered parchment paper, pressing the paper directly on top of the terrine. Tap the pan on a counter to eliminate any air bubbles. Place in a water bath and bake at 360 degrees for 1 hour.

Cool 1 hour or until firm. Unmold and wrap in plastic wrap. Refrigerate 3 hours or overnight. When ready to serve, garnish terrine with green onions and carrot slices cut out with aspic cutters of star or floral shapes. To serve, place some cilantro sauce on a serving plate and arrange 1 slice of terrine over the sauce.

MAKES ABOUT 8 SERVINGS

Cilantro Sauce

1 bunch cilantro, leaves only
1/2 medium onion, peeled and chopped
2 tomatoes, peeled and quartered
1 green pepper, seeded and coarsely chopped
1/2 jalapeño pepper or more to taste, seeded

Combine the cilantro, onion, tomatoes, and peppers in a blender or food processor. Process until smooth.

SOUPS

CUCUMBER SOUP
Velvet Turtle

RED PEPPER SOUP
Rudi Gernreich

ONION SOUP
Jimmy's

GAZPACHO
Scandia

SHRIMP BISQUE
Susan Kranwinkle and Peggy Rahn,
    Inner Gourmet

SOPA DE TORTILLA
Salmagundi

THAI PRAWN SOUP
(Kung Tom Yam)

SAN PEDRO CIOPPINO

VENICE BEACH SEAFOOD SOUP

ORIENTAL TREASURE SOUP

CHINESE FIRE POT

COLD YOGURT GAZPACHO

The bounty of the land and sea has inspired many of the soups that Californians enjoy. Fresh vegetables—onions, red peppers, or cucumbers—might be blended with such aromatic plants as mint or dill in cool yogurt- or buttermilk-based soups. The late Rudi Gernreich, an avant-garde Los Angeles designer of the 1960s, anticipated the new cuisine with his Red Pepper Soup on page 36, featuring a favorite ingredient of the chefs of the 1980s.

From the sea come innovative fish and seafood soups, some hearty, some elegant, owing their inspiration to countries as far flung as France, Spain, Thailand, China, and Italy. One, Oriental Treasure Soup on page 41, is indeed a treasure, made to be served in a chafing dish with an array of exotic ingredients to be added at each diner's option, a sort of low-calorie, Far Eastern fondue. The new California cuisine is imaginative even about its soups.

A tailgate picnic—Broccoli Torte (page 45), Shrimp Bisque (page 37), and Picnic Spinach Salad (page 65)

CUCUMBER SOUP
Velvet Turtle

1 onion, coarsely chopped
1 cup chopped leeks (white part only)
1 large cucumber, peeled, seeded, and diced
4 tablespoons butter or margarine
Salt, pepper
2 tablespoons dry white wine
2 cups water
1½ teaspoons granulated chicken base
2 tablespoons flour
½ cup heavy cream
½ teaspoon lemon juice
5 drops hot pepper sauce
Pinch chopped fresh or dried dill
½ cup half and half, if needed
Sour cream, optional
Lemon wedges for garnish, optional
Minced parsley for garnish, optional

In a soup pot, sauté the onion, leeks, and cucumber, reserving ½ cup diced cucumber, in 2 tablespoons of butter until the onion is transparent. Season to taste with salt and pepper.

Cook and stir until blended. Add the wine, water, and chicken base, and bring to a boil. Melt 2 tablespoons butter in a small pan and blend in the flour; cook for a couple of minutes. Add to the onion mixture and simmer for 1 hour.

In a blender combine the soup for about 15 seconds, then strain it through a fine sieve. Add the cream, lemon juice, pepper sauce, dill, and reserved diced cucumber. Cool soup completely, correct seasoning, and add half and half if soup is too thick. Serve in chilled soup cups. Add ½ teaspoon sour cream to each serving and garnish with lemon wedges and parsley, if desired.

MAKES 6 SERVINGS

RED PEPPER SOUP
Rudi Gernreich

1 cup unsalted butter
2 tablespoons oil
4 cups chopped leeks
6 large red peppers, seeded and sliced
3 cups chicken broth
Salt

6 cups buttermilk
White pepper
Chives or lemon slices, for garnish
Caviar for garnish, optional
10 to 12 green peppers, hollowed out, or any combination of red, green, yellow, and purple peppers

Melt the butter with the oil in a large saucepan. Add the leeks and red peppers. Reduce heat and cook, covered, for 20 minutes or until vegetables are soft. Check occasionally to prevent scorching. Add chicken broth and salt to taste. Simmer, partially covered, over low heat for 30 minutes, or until vegetables are very soft.

Blend pepper mixture in a food processor or blender until smooth. Strain into a large bowl. Stir in the buttermilk and white pepper to taste. Garnish with chives or a thin slice of lemon with a small scoop of caviar centered on the lemon slice, if desired. For single servings, dole the soup into green pepper shells.

MAKES 10 TO 12 SERVINGS

ONION SOUP
Jimmy's

3 tablespoons butter
3 large onions, thinly sliced
2 quarts chicken broth
2 bay leaves
6 black peppercorns
¼ teaspoon whole thyme leaves
Salt, pepper
1 (1-pound, 1¼-ounce) package frozen puff pastry dough, thawed
3 cups shredded Swiss cheese
2 eggs, beaten

Melt the butter in a large saucepan. Add the onion slices and sauté until golden brown. Add the chicken broth. Wrap the bay leaves, peppercorns, and thyme in cheesecloth; tie, and add to the soup. Bring to a boil. Reduce heat, cover, and simmer over medium heat for 30 to 45 minutes. Add salt and pepper to taste. Remove herb bundle.

Roll out the thawed puff pastry dough and cut into 6 thin circles slightly larger than ovenproof soup bowls. Divide half the Swiss cheese into 6 portions. Place one portion in each of the bowls. Fill with the onion soup. Brush the rim and outside edge of each bowl with the beaten eggs. Fit a dough circle on top of each bowl and seal the edges. Brush with remaining egg wash. Sprinkle the remaining cheese over the dough. Bake at 375 degrees for 25 to 30 minutes or until dough puffs and is golden brown.

MAKES 6 SERVINGS

GAZPACHO
Scandia

2 large ripe tomatoes
1/2 large onion
1 small clove garlic
1/2 large cucumber, peeled and sliced
1/2 long green chile pepper
2 cups tomato juice
1/4 cup white wine vinegar
3/4 tablespoon olive oil
1/4 cup dry white wine
1 teaspoon paprika
1/2 teaspoon salt
1/4 teaspoon black pepper
1/4 teaspoon cumin
Few dashes hot pepper sauce
Few dashes Worcestershire sauce
Diced avocado, green pepper, chopped pimiento, chives, and diced, toasted white bread, for garnish

Coarsely chop the tomatoes, onion, garlic, cucumber, and chile pepper. Place in a large bowl, pour tomato juice over, and let stand 2 hours.

Add the vinegar, oil, wine, paprika, salt, pepper, cumin, hot pepper and Worcestershire sauces. Whirl in a blender until smooth. Strain through a sieve and chill several hours. Add cold water if too thick.

Serve in soup cups with additional diced avocado, diced green pepper, chopped pimiento, chopped chives, and diced toasted white bread.

MAKES 8 CUPS

SHRIMP BISQUE
Susan Kranwinkle and Peggy Rahn, Inner Gourmet

3/4 pound shrimp, shelled and deveined
1 tablespoon diced celery
1 tablespoon diced onion
4 medium mushrooms, diced
2 tablespoons butter or margarine
1 tablespoon flour
1 cup chicken broth
1 cup half and half
1/4 teaspoon paprika
Salt
Nutmeg
2 tablespoons dry sherry

Set aside 2 or 3 whole shrimp and dice the rest. Sauté the whole and diced shrimp, celery, onion, and mushrooms in butter until the onion is tender but not brown and the shrimp are cooked. Remove the whole shrimp from the pan and set aside. Add flour to the shrimp-vegetable mixture and cook, stirring, about 1 minute. Add the broth, half and half, and paprika. Season to taste with salt and nutmeg. Cook mixture, stirring, until it becomes smooth and slightly thickened. Stir in the sherry. Top each serving with the reserved whole shrimp.

MAKES 2 TO 3 SERVINGS

SOPA DE TORTILLA
Salmagundi

1 (3-pound) chicken, cut in large pieces
4 quarts water
1 teaspoon celery seeds
1 teaspoon black peppercorns
2 whole cloves garlic, peeled
1 (1-pound) can whole peeled tomatoes, in large chunks
1 green pepper, cut into 1-inch cubes
1 onion, cut into 1-inch cubes
3 sprigs cilantro
1 clove garlic, minced
1/2 teaspoon ground cumin
1/4 teaspoon cayenne pepper
1/4 teaspoon white pepper
1 (10-ounce) package frozen cut corn

TOP: *Cold Yogurt Gazpacho (page 43)*
BOTTOM: *Fresh basil*
LEFT: *San Pedro Cioppino (page 40)*

39

4 green onions, diced
Salt
1 cup cooked rice
4 sprigs parsley, minced
Tortilla chips
Shredded cheddar cheese

Place the chicken, water, celery seeds, peppercorns, and garlic cloves in a large, heavy saucepan. Bring to a boil. Cover, lower heat, and simmer for 35 to 45 minutes or until the chicken is tender. Remove the chicken from the broth. When cool enough to handle, bone and cut into 1-inch pieces. Set aside.

Strain both and return to pot. Add the tomatoes, green pepper, onion, cilantro, minced garlic, cumin, cayenne, and white pepper. Bring to a boil. Reduce heat, cover, and simmer for 30 minutes. Add the corn and green onions, and cook another 10 minutes. Season to taste with salt.

Just before serving, stir in the reserved chicken, rice, and parsley. To serve, spoon the soup into a flameproof tureen or crock. Top with tortilla chips and cheese. Place under broiler, if desired, just until cheese melts.

MAKES 6 TO 8 SERVINGS

THAI PRAWN SOUP
(Kung Tom Yam)

2 pounds fresh large shrimp or prawns, including heads, if available
1 tablespoon oil
1½ teaspoons salt
3 stalks lemon grass, cut into 2-inch pieces
4 citrus leaves or 1 teaspoon chopped lemon peel
Dried kaffir lime peel and leaves, optional
2 fresh red Oriental chiles or jalapeño chiles
1 tablespoon fish sauce
2 or 3 tablespoons lime or lemon juice
1 fresh red chile, for garnish, optional
2 or 3 tablespoons chopped cilantro, for garnish
4 green onions, including tops, chopped, for garnish

Shell and devein the shrimp, reserving heads, tails, and shells. Wash heads and tails well and drain thoroughly. Heat the oil in a large saucepan. Add the heads, tails, and shells, and cook until they turn pink. Add 1 quart water, salt, lemon grass, citrus leaves, kaffir lime peel and leaves, and chiles. Bring to a boil, cover, and simmer for 20 minutes.

Strain the stock and discard any residue. Return the stock to a boil. Add the shrimp and simmer for 3 to 4 minutes until cooked. Add the fish sauce and lemon or lime juice to taste. (The soup should have a sharp, lemony tang.) Seed the red chile and slice. Garnish the soup with chile slices, cilantro, and green onions.

MAKES 8 SERVINGS

SAN PEDRO CIOPPINO

¼ cup olive oil
1 medium onion, chopped
1 clove garlic, minced
1 (1-pound) can whole tomatoes
Salt, pepper
1 tablespoon julienne-cut basil leaves
1 cup dry white wine
1 pound fish fillets, cut into large chunks
½ pound shrimp, shelled and deveined

Heat the oil in a large saucepan or Dutch oven. Add the onion and garlic, and cook until the onion is tender. Add the tomatoes, and their juice, salt and pepper to taste, basil, and 4 cups water. Bring to a boil over high heat. Reduce heat, cover, and simmer for 30 minutes, stirring occasionally.

Add the wine, fish fillets, and more water, if necessary. Return to a boil. Reduce heat, cover, and simmer for 5 minutes, stirring occasionally. Add the shrimp. Cover and simmer for 5 minutes, or until shrimp turn red. Serve in large bowls with French bread, if desired.

MAKES 4 TO 6 SERVINGS

VENICE BEACH SEAFOOD SOUP

Sarasota Fish Soup (recipe follows)
Cooked small pasta shells, at room temperature
Tomatoes, peeled, seeded, and chopped
Black olives, sliced
Cooked shrimp, scallops, or other shellfish or seafood cut into bite-size pieces, at room temperature
Plain or seasoned croutons
Grated Parmesan cheese

Bring the soup to a rolling boil, then transfer it to a chafing dish. Keep the soup at a simmer. Arrange the pasta, tomatoes, olives, fish, croutons, and cheese in bowls, and place them around the chafing dish. It is important for the soup to be very hot, since the addition of the extra ingredients will cool it down quickly. Each person should ladle soup into a bowl and add extra ingredients as desired.

MAKES 8 SERVINGS

Sarasota Fish Soup

2 tablespoons oil
1 cup sliced celery
1 large onion, sliced
2 cloves garlic, sliced
2 pounds fish bones and head
10 black peppercorns
1 teaspoon dried thyme, crumbled
3/4 teaspoon salt
1/2 teaspoon fennel seeds
1 1/2 pounds halibut, cod, or haddock, cut in 1-inch chunks
1 1/2 cups grapefruit juice
1 cup bottled clam juice

Heat the oil in a large, heavy pot and sauté the celery, onion, and garlic until tender. Add the fish bones, 1 quart of water, peppercorns, thyme, salt, and fennel seeds. Bring to a boil, cover, reduce heat, and simmer for 30 minutes. Skim off any scum that rises to the top of the surface. Strain the soup, discard flavorings, and return the soup to the pot. Add the halibut, grapefruit juice, and clam juice. Simmer for 10 minutes or until halibut is cooked.

MAKES 2 QUARTS

ORIENTAL TREASURE SOUP

Far East Chicken Broth (recipe follows)
Diced tofu
Cooked soft Chinese noodles
Sliced green onions
Sliced fresh mushrooms
Sliced water chestnuts
Celery, cut into 1-inch-long julienne strips
Sweet red peppers, cut into 1-inch-long julienne strips
Cilantro leaves, for garnish

Bring the broth to a rolling boil and place in a chafing dish over a heating unit and keep it at a simmer. Arrange the tofu, noodles, green onions, mushrooms, water chestnuts, celery, and red peppers in bowls around the chafing dish. Ladle the broth into soup bowls and let guests add ingredients of their choice. (Keep broth very hot, as the addition of extra ingredients will quickly cool it.) Garnish with cilantro leaves.

Far East Chicken Broth

2 (2 1/2- to 3-pound) chickens
2 medium onions, sliced
4 ribs celery, chopped
2 carrots, cut into chunks
4 sprigs parsley
1 teaspoon salt
1/4 teaspoon white pepper
3 tablespoons soy sauce
1 1/2 tablespoons dry sherry
1 1/2 teaspoons ginger juice (see note)
1 1/2 teaspoons sesame oil

Place the chickens in a large, heavy pot. Add 2 quarts water, onions, celery, carrots, parsley, salt, and white pepper, and bring to a boil. Skim off any scum that rises to the top. Cover, reduce heat, and simmer 1 1/2 to 2 hours or until the chickens are very tender.

Remove chickens from pot and set aside. Strain broth. There should be about 7 cups. Return the broth to the pot and add soy sauce, sherry, ginger juice, and sesame oil. Strip chicken from bones and dice. Add to broth and bring once more to a boil.

MAKES ABOUT 2 1/2 QUARTS SOUP

Note: Ginger juice can be obtained by pressing 6 to 8 peeled and diced slices of fresh ginger in a garlic press.

CHINESE FIRE POT

1 pound boneless beef sirloin or round
1 pound boned chicken breasts
1 pound fish fillets
1/2 to 1 pound medium shrimp
1 pound Chinese cabbage
1/2 pound fresh forest mushrooms or cultivated mushrooms
Lemon juice

2 (3½-ounce) packages enoki mushrooms
¾ pound Chinese snow peas
2 bunches green onions
2 bunches spinach
1 (8-ounce) can water chestnuts, drained and sliced
1 (8-ounce) can bamboo shoots, drained and sliced
4 (13¾-ounce) cans chicken broth
Sweet-and-sour sauce
Soy sauce
Prepared hot Chinese mustard
¼ pound fine egg noodles, cooked
Chopped cilantro or chives for garnish, optional

Place the beef, chicken, and fish in the freezer and chill until firm to the touch but not frozen. Slice the beef and chicken in strips ¼-inch thick and about 2 inches long. Cut the fish into ¾-inch cubes. Shell and devein the shrimp. Chop the cabbage into bite-size chunks. Clean the mushrooms. If using forest mushrooms, remove and discard stems. Slice the mushrooms and sprinkle with lemon juice. Cut off and discard the root portion of the enoki mushrooms and separate the clusters as much as possible. Wash, trim ends , and string the pea pods. Clean the green onions and cut in half lengthwise, including the green portion. Cut into 2-inch lengths. Clean the spinach and discard the thick stems.

To serve, arrange the beef, chicken, fish, shrimp, cabbage, forest mushrooms, enoki mushrooms, snow peas, green onions, spinach leaves, water chestnuts, and bamboo shoots in individual rows on large platters or serving plates. Bring the broth to a boil. Place a heating unit under a Chinese hot pot and pour the boiling broth into the hot-pot bowl.

Using a Chinese wire ladle and chopsticks or fondue forks, each person places whatever ingredients are desired into the hot broth to poach. When cooked (this will take only a few moments), the ingredients are then dipped into the sweet-and-sour sauce, soy sauce, or hot mustard as desired, and eaten.

MAKES 6 TO 8 SERVINGS

Note: It is not necessary to use all of the ingredients listed here as long as you make sure to offer an interesting blend of meats, fish, and vegetables. Other meats and vegetables can be substituted if desired.

COLD YOGURT GAZPACHO

3 medium cucumbers
6 cups yogurt
2 tablespoons white vinegar
1 tablespoon olive oil
3 cloves garlic, minced
1 tablespoon finely chopped mint
1½ teaspoons finely chopped dill
Salt

Peel the cucumbers and slice lengthwise into halves. Scoop out the seeds from each half with a spoon. Coarsely grate the cucumbers. There should be about 3 cups.

Place the yogurt in a deep bowl and whisk or stir until completely smooth. Gently but thoroughly stir in the grated cucumbers, vinegar, oil, garlic, mint, and dill. Season to taste with salt. Do not overbeat.

Refrigerate the soup for 2 hours or until thoroughly chilled. Place an ice cube in each serving. Top with desired condiments.

MAKES 2 TO 2½ QUARTS

Makings for Chinese Fire Pot soup (page 41)

VEGETABLES

ARTICHOKE VINAIGRETTE
Tutto Italia

COLD POACHED ASPARAGUS WITH FLAVORED
    MAYONNAISE
Narsai's, Berkeley

BROCCOLI TORTE
Susan Kranwinkle and Peggy Rahn, Inner Gourmet

CARROT-MUSHROOM RAGOUT
Roland Gibert, Bernard's

GRILLED JAPANESE EGGPLANTS
Elka Gilmore, Camelions

MAUI ONION RINGS
Michael's

ONION CAKES
Henry Chung, The Hunan Restaurant, San Francisco

SALT-ROASTED POTATOES
Gary Danko, Beringer Vineyards

VINE-RIPENED TOMATOES STUFFED WITH SUGAR
    SNAP PEAS
Patrick Healy, Colette, Beverly Pavilion Hotel

STUFFED ZUCCHINI FLOWERS
Ken Frank, La Toque

SMALL STUFFED VEGETABLES WITH SHRIMP
    RATATOUILLE AND TWO SAUCES
Joachim Splichal, Max au Triangle

VEGETABLES À LA GRECQUE
Club Culinaire Français de Californie, Los Angeles

RAGOUT OF BABY VEGETABLES
Roland Gibert, Bernard's

VEGETABLE CHILI
Gelson's Market

CHINESE ASPARAGUS SAUTÉ

SHIITAKE SAUTÉ

CORN PUDDING

EGGPLANT STACKS

LEEKS AU GRATIN

JALAPEÑO JELLY

DRIED TOMATOES

What a gift nature bestowed when it placed California in a temperate zone! It also provided an amazing range of subclimates that help supply the nation—and the world—with the land's bounty and that inspired experimental horticulturalists to develop exotic and unusual hybrids never seen before.

California's cornucopia of plenty keeps pouring forth produce the year round, creating a broader market at lower prices. At one time the nouvelle cuisine's experiments with baby vegetables (picked before maturity) were available only to the privileged few who could search out and afford the rare and costly produce, some of it experimental hybrids.

Today the increasingly sophisticated consumer provides a ready market for unusual produce. These pages contain many delightful culinary experiments with California's vegetables. There is the wonderful Ragout of Baby Vegetables on page 52 that can be made in ten minutes. It uses tiny eggplant, infant squashes—from zucchini to patty pan—all grown now in California.

Then there are zucchini flowers stuffed with a mixture that includes mushrooms, mint, and garlic, fried in a beer batter (page 49), a great recent favorite. Much of our asparagus, a leading crop in Imperial Valley where sunshine streams over fertile soil during the winter months, is air-shipped to European restaurants and markets. You will find two speedy and exotic ways to prepare this most elegant vegetable on pages 45 and 53.

These days vegetables have a place of honor on our menus and are no longer considered uninteresting also-rans.

ARTICHOKE VINAIGRETTE
Tutto Italia

4 extra-large artichokes
2 cups concentrated lemon juice
1 tablespoon salt
Pinch black pepper
Pinch oregano
Pinch crushed red pepper flakes
Vinaigrette (recipe follows)

Trim artichokes stems to ½ inch. Place upright in a large kettle and add enough water to cover. Add the lemon juice, salt, pepper, oregano, and red pepper flakes. Bring to a boil, reduce heat, and simmer for about 1 hour or until leaves pull easily from the base of the artichokes. Remove from pan and invert artichokes to drain thoroughly and cool. Using a spoon, remove the chokes and discard.

Stand artichokes upright in a serving dish. Place a few tablespoons of vinaigrette in the cavity of each artichoke. Chill. Serve with remaining vinaigrette.

MAKES 4 SERVINGS

Vinaigrette

1 cup olive oil
½ cup white wine vinegar
Salt, pepper
3 cloves garlic, peeled and crushed
Pinch oregano
Pinch crushed red pepper flakes
1 tablespoon capers
2 tablespoons chopped pimiento

Combine the oil, vinegar, salt, pepper, garlic, oregano, red pepper flakes, capers, and pimiento in a medium bowl. Blend well.

MAKES ABOUT 1½ CUPS

COLD POACHED ASPARAGUS WITH FLAVORED MAYONNAISE
Narsai's, Berkeley

1½ pounds asparagus
1 cup mayonnaise
2 tablespoons steak sauce or to taste

Trim the tough ends from the asparagus. Place the asparagus in a steamer rack over simmering water. Cover and steam until asparagus is crisp-tender, about 5 to 10 minutes, depending on size of asparagus.

Place the mayonnaise in a small bowl. Add steak sauce and blend well. Serve with the asparagus.

MAKES 6 TO 8 SERVINGS

BROCCOLI TORTE
Susan Kranwinkle and Peggy Rahn,
Inner Gourmet

2 small onions, chopped
½ cup butter or margarine
½ cup flour
1 cup milk
4 eggs, separated
1½ cups puréed cooked broccoli or 2 (10-ounce) packages
    frozen broccoli, drained and puréed
Salt, pepper
½ cup grated Parmesan cheese
2 tablespoons bread crumbs
½ pound bratwurst
4 German pickles or kosher dills
½ cup mayonnaise
1 cup sour cream

Sauté half the onions in butter until soft but not brown. Add the flour and cook, stirring, for 2 minutes, until flour is lightly browned. Add the milk and cook, stirring, until sauce is smooth. Set aside to cool.

Beat the egg yolks, then stir a small amount of the onion sauce into them. Add the rest of the onion sauce and stir to blend. Add the broccoli and season to taste with salt and pepper. Beat the egg whites until stiff and fold into the broccoli mixture. Stir in the Parmesan cheese.

Grease two 9-inch round baking pans and cover the bottoms with wax paper. Sprinkle 1 tablespoon bread crumbs over the bottom of each. Divide the broccoli mixture between pans. Bake at 350 degrees for 15 to 20 minutes, until mixture pulls away from sides of pan slightly. Cool, and remove from pans.

Remove casings from bratwurst, and sauté them with the remaining onions. Place the mixture in a food processor with the pickles and chop fine. Blend in the mayonnaise. Season to taste with salt and pepper. Cool.

Spread the cooled sausage filling over 1 broccoli layer; top with the second broccoli layer. Coat the top and sides of the torte with sour cream and chill thoroughly.

MAKES 8 TO 12 SERVINGS

CARROT-MUSHROOM RAGOUT
Roland Gibert, Bernard's

¼ cup butter
¾ pound baby turnips, with ½-inch stems
¾ pound baby carrots, with ½-inch stems
¼ pound button mushrooms
¼ pound oyster mushrooms, sliced
¼ pound shiitake mushrooms, sliced
½ pound arugula, mâche, or red leaf lettuce
6 pear tomatoes
Salt, white pepper
2 tablespoons fresh tarragon, or 1 teaspoon dried

Melt the butter in a large saucepan. Add the turnips and carrots, toss, cover, and cook 4 minutes. Add the mushrooms and sauté 2 to 3 minutes. Add arugula or other greens, pear tomatoes, and season to taste with salt and pepper. Sauté 2 minutes, shaking pan, until vegetables barely wilt. Sprinkle with tarragon.

MAKES 8 SERVINGS

GRILLED JAPANESE EGGPLANTS
Elka Gilmore, Camelions

1 clove garlic
2 tablespoons olive oil
Salt, white pepper
1 tablespoon chopped fresh basil
16 Japanese eggplants, split lengthwise
1 red pepper
1 green or yellow pepper
¼ cup chopped fresh herbs (basil, oregano, thyme)
8 ½-inch-thick medallions California or French goat cheese
½ cup walnut pieces
1 tablespoon butter
1 tablespoon brown sugar
Cayenne pepper
Balsamic Dressing (recipe follows)

Combine the garlic, olive oil, salt and white pepper to taste, and basil in a shallow pan. Place the eggplants split side down in the marinade; turn several times to coat well. Let marinate for 20 minutes. Grill the eggplants split side down on a grill over medium coals. Set aside when done.

Roast the peppers on the grill until charred. Place in a plastic bag until cool enough to peel. Under cold running water, peel off charred portions of skin. Cut peppers into eighths, discarding seeds. Set aside.

Press the herbs onto the goat cheese medallions. Heat at 350 degrees for 3 minutes until warmed.

Sauté the walnuts in butter. Toss with brown sugar, cayenne, and a pinch of salt. Set aside.

Arrange 4 eggplant halves on each plate, and place 2 strips each of red and green peppers between the eggplant halves. Set 2 cheese medallions beside the peppers. Sprinkle sautéed walnuts over top. Drizzle dressing over the salad.

MAKES 8 SERVINGS

Balsamic Dressing

2 tablespoons balsamic vinegar or fresh lemon juice
¼ cup virgin olive oil
Salt, pepper

Combine the vinegar, oil, and salt and pepper to taste.

Grilled foods—Grilled Japanese Eggplants (recipe above); Roy Yamaguchi's Grilled Prawn Salad (page 71)

Maui Onion Rings
Michael's

1¼ cups flour
1 tablespoon cornstarch
Salt, cracked black pepper
1 (12-ounce) bottle Killian's red ale or other ale
3 Maui onions
Oil for deep frying

Combine the flour, cornstarch, and salt and pepper to taste in a large bowl. Whisk in the ale until smooth. Cut the onions into ¼- to ⅓-inch-thick slices. Coat with the batter.

Heat oil in deep fryer to 400 degrees. Gently add the onion rings to the hot oil without crowding the pan, and cook until golden brown. Remove with a slotted spoon and drain on paper towels.

MAKES 4 TO 6 SERVINGS

Onion Cakes
Henry Chung, The Hunan Restaurant, San Francisco

8 flour tortillas
2 tablespoons sesame oil
1 egg, lightly beaten
½ cup finely chopped green onions
Oil for deep frying
Salt

Brush 4 tortillas with sesame oil, then some of the egg. Sprinkle about 2 tablespoons green onions over each tortilla. Top each with the remaining tortillas. Press firmly around edges, and cover with plastic wrap. Let stand until ready to deep fry.

Heat oil for deep-frying in a wok or deep pan to 400 degrees. Using tongs, slip the tortilla cakes into the hot oil. Cook, turning with tongs, to brown both sides. Drain the tortilla, holding it vertically over the pan. Drain again on paper towels. While hot, cut each tortilla into 4 to 8 wedges. Sprinkle lightly with salt. Serve hot.

MAKES 4 ONION CAKES

Salt-Roasted Potatoes
Gary Danko, Beringer Vineyards

12 small new potatoes
¼ cup olive oil
½ teaspoon salt
¼ teaspoon pepper

Cook new potatoes in boiling water until just tender, 15 to 20 minutes. Do not overcook. Rub with olive oil and roll in the salt and pepper.

Place on a grill over medium coals and grill until skin is crisp, about 10 to 12 minutes. Alternatively, roast in a 400-degree oven for about 10 to 12 minutes.

MAKES 6 SERVINGS

Vine-Ripened Tomatoes Stuffed with Sugar Snap Peas
Patrick Healy, Colette, Beverly Pavilion Hotel

1 onion, chopped
2 tablespoons butter
1 tablespoon chopped fresh mint leaves plus whole mint leaves, for garnish
1 cup shelled sugar snap peas
Pinch nutmeg
Salt, dash white pepper
6 small vine-ripened tomatoes

Sauté the onion in butter until tender. Add the chopped mint leaves and peas. Sauté 1 minute. Add nutmeg, salt, and pepper. Cut a thin slice from the stem end of each tomato. Hollow the tomato, leaving the shell intact. Season with salt and pepper, if desired. Stuff the tomato shells with pea mixture. Place a tomato cap beside each filled tomato. Garnish with mint leaves.

MAKES 6 SERVINGS

STUFFED ZUCCHINI FLOWERS
Ken Frank, La Toque

Spinach
Napa cabbage
Mushrooms
Celery
Carrot, peeled
1 tablespoon chopped fresh mint
1 clove garlic, chopped
Sesame oil
Salt, pepper
Zucchini flowers, 12 to 18 depending on size
Peanut oil for deep frying
Beer Batter (recipe follows)

Dice enough spinach, Napa cabbage, mushrooms, celery, and carrot to make 2 cups. Add mint leaves and garlic. Heat about 2 tablespoons sesame oil in a large skillet. Add the vegetable mixture and cook just until wilted. Season to taste with salt and pepper.

Rinse the zucchini flowers. Stuff each flower with about 1 tablespoon of the vegetable mixture, depending on the size of the flower. Twist ends to seal. Heat peanut oil in a deep skillet to 360 degrees. Dip stuffed flowers into beer batter, allowing excess batter to drain. Cook in the hot oil until golden brown, about 3 minutes.

MAKES 6 SERVINGS

Beer Batter

1⅓ cups flour
1 teaspoon sugar
¼ teaspoon white pepper
1 tablespoon oil
3 egg whites
1 cup beer
Pinch salt
Dash sesame oil

Combine the flour, sugar, pepper, oil, and egg whites. Mix well. Add the beer, salt, and sesame oil. Chill.

MAKES ABOUT 2 CUPS

SMALL STUFFED VEGETABLES WITH SHRIMP RATATOUILLE AND TWO SAUCES
Joachim Splichal, Max au Triangle

4 zucchini flowers
4 cherry tomatoes
4 baby corn squash (see note)
Shrimp Ratatouille (recipe follows)
Raw Yellow Tomato Sauce (recipe page 52)
Raw Tomato Sauce (recipe page 52)
Chopped fresh basil, optional

Blanch the zucchini flowers, cherry tomatoes, and corn squash by cooking in rapidly boiling salted water for 1 minute. Remove with a slotted spoon and drain. When cool enough to handle, peel the tomatoes and squash. Halve the tomatoes and gently hollow out the centers; likewise hollow the squash.

Stuff the zucchini flowers, cherry tomatoes, and corn squash with the shrimp ratatouille. Place the stuffed vegetables in a greased baking pan and bake at 350 degrees for 10 to 15 minutes.

Spoon the yellow tomato sauce on one side of each plate, and the raw tomato sauce on the other side. Sprinkle chopped fresh basil down the center if desired. Arrange the stuffed vegetables on the plates.

MAKES 4 SERVINGS

Note: Corn squash are tiny corn-shaped yellow zucchini and are available at some gourmet vegetable markets. Substitute small green zucchini if necessary.

Shrimp Ratatouille

¼ small Japanese eggplant, finely diced
¼ tomato, finely diced
¼ zucchini, finely diced
1 shallot, finely diced
1 small clove garlic, minced
¼ red pepper, finely diced
Olive oil
2 basil leaves, cut into fine julienne slices
10 Santa Barbara shrimp, shelled, deveined, and diced

Sauté the eggplant, tomato, zucchini, shallot, garlic, and red pepper in 2 tablespoons olive oil. Add the basil. Remove the vegetable mixture from the pan and set aside. Add up to 1

TOP: *Joachim Splichal*

BOTTOM: *Zucchini blossom*

RIGHT: *Small Stuffed Vegetables with Shrimp Ratatouille and Two Sauces (page 49)*

tablespoon oil if necessary to the pan for cooking the shrimp. Heat the oil and add the shrimp; sauté until they turn red. Do not overcook. Remove the shrimp from the pan and combine with the vegetable mixture. Season to taste with salt.

Raw Yellow Tomato Sauce

2 ripe yellow tomatoes (see note)
3 tablespoons olive oil
5 basil leaves, cut into julienne slices
Salt

Plunge the tomatoes in boiling water and boil for 1 minute. Peel and seed. Purée in a food processor or blender. Stir in the olive oil, basil, and season with salt.

MAKES ABOUT ½ CUP SAUCE

Note: Yellow tomatoes are found at some gourmet food stores.

Raw Tomato Sauce

2 ripe tomatoes
3 tablespoons olive oil
5 basil leaves, cut into julienne slices
Salt

Plunge the tomatoes in boiling water and boil for 1 minute. Peel and seed. Purée in a food processor or blender. Stir in the olive oil, basil, and season with salt.

MAKES ABOUT ½ CUP SAUCE

Vegetables à la Grecque
Club Culinaire Français de Californie, Los Angeles

2 tablespoons olive oil
½ cup chopped onion
1 clove garlic, minced
2 tablespoons tomato paste
2 large tomatoes, diced
¼ cup dry white wine
½ teaspoon ground coriander

Chopped parsley
Salt, pepper
3 zucchini, sliced
3 Japanese eggplants, sliced
6 tiny artichokes, cleaned and leaves trimmed, optional
1 small cauliflower, broken into florets

Heat the oil in a skillet. Add the onion and garlic. Cook, stirring, until onion is tender. Stir in the tomato paste. Cook, stirring, to blend with onion. Add the tomatoes, wine, coriander, and parsley, and season to taste with salt and pepper. Cook for 30 minutes, stirring occasionally.

Place the tomato mixture in a food processor or blender and purée. Return to skillet. Add the zucchini, eggplants, artichokes, and cauliflower. Bring to a boil, reduce heat, and cook over low heat for 20 minutes or until vegetables are tender-crisp.

MAKES 8 SERVINGS

Ragout of Baby Vegetables
Roland Gibert, Bernard's

¼ cup butter
2 ½ to 3 ounces ham, prosciutto, or roast duck, diced
1 large onion, peeled and chopped
4 medium tomatoes, peeled, seeded, and chopped
¾ pound baby eggplant
¾ pound baby zucchini
¾ pound baby yellow squash
¾ pound baby patty pan squash
8 pear tomatoes
1 bay leaf
Few sprigs fresh thyme, or dried
2 cloves garlic, unpeeled
Sea salt, white pepper
2 tablespoons chopped fresh tarragon, or 1 teaspoon dried

Melt the butter in a large saucepan. Add the ham and onion and sauté until the ham is well done and the onion is golden. Add the tomatoes and sauté 2 minutes. Add the eggplant whole, if small, or cut in halves or quarters, and sauté 2 minutes. Add the zucchini and yellow squash and sauté 2 minutes. (If the squash are not small, halve or quarter them.) Add the patty pan squash and sauté another 2 minutes. Add the pear tomatoes, bay leaf, thyme, garlic, and season to taste with sea salt and white pepper. Cover and simmer over very low heat to prevent vegetables from drying and scorching, about 10 minutes, or until vegetables are tender but firm. Discard the bay leaf, thyme sprigs, and garlic cloves. Turn onto a serving platter and sprinkle with tarragon.

MAKES 8 SERVINGS

Vegetable Chili
Gelson's Market

½ cup dry kidney beans
¼ cup bulgur
½ cup olive oil
1 small red onion, cubed
1 small sweet white onion, cubed
1½ tablespoons minced garlic
½ cup cubed celery
½ cup cubed carrots
2 tablespoons chili powder
2 tablespoons cumin
½ teaspoon cayenne pepper
1 tablespoon chopped fresh basil
1 tablespoon chopped fresh oregano
1 yellow squash, cubed
1 zucchini, cubed
1 green pepper, cubed
1 red pepper, cubed
1 cup sliced mushrooms
½ cup cubed tomatoes
½ cup tomato paste
¾ cup white wine
Salt, pepper

Soak the beans in cold water to cover overnight. Drain off water. Add 3 cups fresh water to beans and cook over medium heat until tender, about 45 minutes. Drain beans, reserving cooking liquid.

Bring ½ cup water to a boil. Pour over the bulgur in a bowl. Let stand for 30 minutes to soften the wheat (the water will be absorbed).

Heat the olive oil in a large saucepan. Add the red and sweet white onions, and sauté until tender. Add the garlic, celery, and carrots. Sauté until glazed. Add the chili powder, cumin, cayenne, basil, and oregano. Cook over low heat until the carrots are almost tender. Add the squash, zucchini, green and red peppers and mushrooms, and cook 4 minutes. Stir in the bulgur, kidney beans, tomatoes, and reserved

cooking liquid from the beans. Cook for 30 minutes or until the vegetables are tender. Mix the tomato paste with white wine until smooth, then stir into the vegetable mixture. Season to taste with salt and pepper.

MAKES 6 TO 8 SERVINGS

Chinese Asparagus Sauté

1 pound asparagus
2 to 3 tablespoons peanut oil
¾ pound raw shrimp, peeled and deveined
5 mushrooms, sliced
2 teaspoons cornstarch
¼ cup chicken or vegetable broth (water may be substituted)
2 tablespoons soy sauce
1 tablespoon mirin or sherry
Pinch sugar
Salt, pepper

Break off the woody ends from the asparagus and cut the spears into ½-inch diagonal slices. Heat half the oil in a wok or skillet and cook the asparagus until it turns bright green. Push the asparagus to one side, add the remaining oil, and sauté the shrimp and mushrooms for 2 minutes.

In a bowl combine the cornstarch, broth, soy sauce, mirin, and sugar. Stir into the asparagus mixture. Season to taste with salt and pepper. Cook 1 to 2 minutes longer.

MAKES 4 SERVINGS

Shiitake Sauté

8 large fresh shiitake mushrooms
2 tablespoons vegetable oil
1 tablespoon mirin or sweet sherry
1 tablespoon soy sauce
½ teaspoon sugar

Cut off the mushroom stems, and cut the caps into wedges. Heat the oil in a skillet. Add the mushrooms and stir-fry until almost tender. Add the mirin, soy sauce, and sugar, and toss to coat mushrooms.

MAKES 8 SERVINGS

Dried Tomatoes (page 57)

CORN PUDDING

4 eggs
1 tablespoon flour
1 tablespoon sugar
2½ cups milk
1 cup fresh whole kernel corn, or frozen
Pinch nutmeg or mace
1 tablespoon butter, melted

Beat the eggs well. Blend in the flour, sugar, and milk. Stir in the corn, nutmeg, and butter. Pour into a 1½-quart baking dish and bake at 350 degrees for 15 minutes. Stir and bake 30 minutes longer or until custard is set.

MAKES ABOUT 4 SERVINGS

EGGPLANT STACKS

2 small eggplants
6 to 8 slices onion, cut ½-inch thick
Juice of ½ lemon
6 to 8 slices tomato, cut ½-inch thick
Cheese Sauce (recipe follows)
Salt, pepper
2 onions, thinly sliced
1 tablespoon oil
1 tablespoon butter or margarine
2 tablespoons chopped parsley

Cut each eggplant crosswise into three or four 1-inch-thick slices, including the bottom and stem end. Slice the bottom so that it is level. Parboil the eggplant and ½-inch onion slices in a small amount of water to which lemon juice has been added. Cover and cook for 5 minutes. Turn eggplant slices at halfway point in cooking. Drain on paper towels. Place the bottom eggplant slices side by side in a 9-inch-square baking dish. Top each with 1 parboiled onion slice and 1 tomato slice, and spoon over ¼ cup cheese sauce. Season to taste with salt and pepper. Cover with next largest eggplant slice and repeat stacking with onion slices, tomato slices, cheese sauce, and salt and pepper to taste. Top each with its stem end.

To hold layers in place, insert 2 or 3 long bamboo skewers lengthwise through each eggplant stack. Sauté thinly sliced onions in oil and butter in a large heavy skillet until transparent. Season to taste with salt and pepper. Spoon onions around eggplant in baking dish. Sprinkle with parsley. Bake at 350 degrees 20 to 25 minutes or until vegetables are tender. If necessary, add a small amount of water to the pan to keep onions from scorching. Remove skewers, and slice lengthwise into wedges to serve. Serve additional cheese sauce on side.

MAKES 4 TO 6 SERVINGS

Cheese Sauce

2 tablespoons butter or margarine
2 tablespoons flour
¼ teaspoon dry mustard
2 cups milk
2 cups shredded cheddar cheese
Salt, white pepper
Hot pepper sauce

Melt the butter in a small saucepan. Blend in the flour and mustard. Stir in milk until smooth. Bring to a boil, stirring constantly. Cook, stirring, until thickened, about 1 minute. Stir in cheese until melted. Season to taste with salt, pepper, and hot pepper sauce.

MAKES 2½ CUPS

LEEKS AU GRATIN

2 bunches baby or small leeks
Black pepper
½ cup grated Parmesan cheese

Wash and trim leeks; leave whole. Cook in a large saucepan of boiling salted water, covered, for 15 minutes. Drain. Preheat broiler. Arrange in a buttered baking dish. Season to taste with pepper. Add the grated cheese, then heat under the broiler until cheese is melted.

MAKES 6 TO 8 SERVINGS

JALAPEÑO JELLY

³/4 cup ground green peppers
¹/2 cup ground jalapeño chiles
6 cups sugar
1¹/2 cups cider vinegar
1 (6-ounce) bottle liquid pectin
Green food color

Remove seeds before grinding green peppers and chiles. Grind, using the fine blade of a meat grinder or use a food processor. Mix the green peppers, chiles, sugar, and vinegar, and bring to a rolling boil. Boil for 1 minute. Remove from heat and allow to cool slightly. Add pectin and 4 or 5 drops of food color. Mix well. Strain into hot sterilized jars and seal.

MAKES ABOUT 6 HALF-PINTS

Note: If your skin is sensitive, wear protective gloves when handling peppers and chiles.

DRIED TOMATOES

3 pounds firm ripe Italian or plum tomatoes (Romas)
¹/2 teaspoon herb seasoning (oregano, basil, or any herb combination) per tomato
1 teaspoon minced garlic
Salt, optional
2 rosemary sprigs or 1 tablespoon dried rosemary leaves, optional
1¹/4 cups olive oil, approximately

Choose tomatoes with even red color, and without any green or black spots. Wash tomatoes, removing stem ends. Slice lengthwise in halves. Squeeze gently to remove some of the juice and seeds. Pat dry. Sprinkle with herbs, garlic, and salt to taste. Dry tomatoes, using oven or sun-drying method given below, until about two-thirds dry.

To prevent molding, loosely pack the dried tomatoes in a 1- to 1¹/2-pint jar with rosemary sprigs right away. Pour in olive oil to cover tomatoes. Cover jars and store airtight in a cool, dark, dry area or in the refrigerator, in which case the olive oil will be cloudy. Use immediately or let stand 1¹/2 months for flavors to develop more fully. Tomatoes will stay fresh as long as oil tastes fresh.

MAKES ABOUT 1 PINT DRIED TOMATOES

Oven-Drying Method: Place prepared tomato halves, cut side down, on non-stick pans (do not use foil). Or, arrange tomatoes on wire racks placed on pans. Bake at 300 degrees for 3 to 5 hours or until dried. (Avoid overdrying as that makes tomatoes tough. But if not dried enough, tomatoes will mold.)

Sun-Drying Method: This method is best used in hot weather with relatively low humidity. Use shallow wood-framed trays with nylon netting, cheesecloth, or screen bottoms. Place the prepared tomatoes cut side down, on trays. Cover trays with protective netting and place on blocks, bricks, or a slat-like platform raised from the ground in direct sun. There should be air circulating under the food.

Dry tomatoes for about 3 days, turning after half that time, to expose cut halves to the sun. Bring the trays into the house or place in a sheltered spot outdoors before the dew rises after sundown.

OVERLEAF: *Assortment of olive oils*

SALADS

SUMMER VEGETABLE PLATE
Patrick Healy, Colette, Beverly Pavilion Hotel

BAKED GOAT CHEESE WITH GARDEN SALAD
Alice Waters, Chez Panisse, Berkeley

GRILLED EGGPLANT SALAD
Wolfgang Puck, Spago

GRILLED RADICCHIO SALAD
Le St. Germain

RADICCHIO AND BEAN SALAD
Rex Il Ristorante

WARM VEGETABLE SALAD WITH TRUFFLES
Patrick Terrail, Ma Maison

PORTABLE PICNIC SPINACH SALAD
Susan Kranwinkle and Peggy Rahn, Inner Gourmet

SALADE MIKADO WITH TARRAGON VINAIGRETTE
Werner Albrecht, Five-Star Catering Co., Inc.

ASPERGES AUX ARROWROOT VINAIGRETTE DE PRUNE
(Asparagus in a Blanket with Plum Vinaigrette)
Susumu Fukui, La Petite Chaya

ITALIAN SALAD
Claudio Marchesan, Prego

GREEN BEAN NEST WITH SCALLOP EGGS
Janet Trefethen, Trefethen Vineyards

WARM SCALLOP SALAD WITH ROASTED RED PEPPERS
Gary Danko, Beringer Vineyards

PAPAYA WITH SHRIMP PIQUANT
Susan Kranwinkle and Peggy Rahn, Inner Gourmet

GRILLED PRAWN SALAD
Roy Yamaguchi, 385 North

ABALONE SALAD
Wolfgang Puck, Chinois on Main

SNAPPER SALAD
Michael's

TRUMPS SEAFOOD SALAD FOR ONE
Michael Roberts, Trumps

FIDDLEHEAD FERN AND SMOKED CHICKEN SALAD
Michael Roberts, Trumps

GYOZA DUCK SALAD
Roy Yamaguchi, 385 North

SZECHUAN NOODLE SALAD IN PEANUT SAUCE
Hugh Carpenter

PICNIC VEGETABLE SALAD

COMPOSED CALIFORNIA CORN SALAD

AVOCADO CHEF SALAD

HAWAIIAN CHICKEN SALAD

MAI FUN CHICKEN SALAD

SPANISH CHICKEN SALAD

Long before the new California cuisine achieved its recent eminence, the remarkably varied salads served here in restaurants and homes had already earned a special fame for the region's gastronomy. "California" and "salad" were practically synonymous. Our way of life calls for foods that can be enjoyed informally, outdoors as well as indoors, and the wealth of beautiful fresh produce available year-round answers that call with the makings for salads that are often one-dish meals.

At Beringer Vineyards, guests are regaled with a Warm Scallop Salad with Roasted Red Peppers (page 69) prepared with the vineyard's own sauvignon blanc (fumé blanc). The rolling hills of Napa and Sonoma valleys are famous not only for their wines but for the hospitality of the winegrowers who produce incredibly beautiful meals using products of the land around them.

SUMMER VEGETABLE PLATE
Patrick Healy, Colette, Beverly Pavilion Hotel

6 baby turnips (see note)
6 baby carrots
Salt, white pepper
Butter Wash (recipe follows)
6 baby artichoke bottoms
¼ pound snow peas
6 baby beets
Radicchio hearts
Butter
Zucchini Boats (recipe follows)

Bring a large saucepan of salted water to a boil. Add the turnips and carrots and cook in boiling water until tender but firm, about 3 to 5 minutes depending on size. Remove from cooking water, season to taste with salt and pepper, and brush with the butter wash. Set aside. Do not discard the cooking water.

Repeat process separately with the artichoke bottoms, snow peas, and beets in the cooking water only until each is tender, but still firm. Brush the vegetables with the butter wash after they are cooked. Season to taste with salt and pepper. Set aside.

When ready to serve, arrange a few turnips, carrots, beets, artichoke bottoms, snow peas, radicchio hearts, and zucchini boats either on a large serving platter or individual plates. Season to taste with salt and pepper.

Note: Peel the whole baby vegetables, but leave ¹/2-inch stem intact. Clean carefully around the stem.

Butter Wash

¼ cup butter, melted
1 tablespoon water

Mix melted butter with water.

Zucchini Boats

2 or 3 zucchini, about 1 inch in diameter
Salt, white pepper
Butter Wash
Filling for zucchini boats

Cut the ends off the zucchini and hollow. Cook in boiling salted water until tender but still firm, about 2 minutes. Drain. Season with salt and pepper and brush with butter wash. Cut zucchini into 2-inch rounds. Fill the zucchini boats with any desired filling, such as chopped vegetables, seafood, poultry or meat salad, ratatouille, or egg mixtures.

BAKED GOAT CHEESE WITH GARDEN SALAD
Alice Waters, Chez Panisse, Berkeley

4 (¹/2-inch-thick) rounds fresh log chèvre, 8 ounces
3 to 4 thyme sprigs
Olive oil
1 cup fine dried bread crumbs
1 teaspoon dried thyme
2 to 3 tablespoons red wine vinegar
Salt, pepper
¹/2 head rocket, lamb's lettuce, or small oak leaf and red leaf lettuces, or chervil
1 day-old baguette
¹/2 cup butter, melted
2 to 3 cloves garlic, split

Place goat cheese rounds and the fresh thyme in a shallow pan. Sprinkle with ¼ cup olive oil. Marinate for up to 1 day. Mix together the bread crumbs and dried thyme. Set aside. Make a dressing with ¹/2 cup olive oil, vinegar, and salt and pepper to taste. Set aside. Wash and dry lettuces.

Slice the baguette into twenty-four ¼-inch-thick slices. Brush each slice with some of the melted butter. Place on a baking sheet and bake at 350 degrees for 5 to 7 minutes, or until croutons are lightly browned. While still warm rub each crouton with a cut clove of garlic.

Dip the marinated cheese slices in the bread crumbs. Place in a lightly oiled baking dish. Bake at 400 degrees for 6 minutes, or until cheese is barely bubbling and is golden brown. Toss lettuces with enough dressing to lightly coat. Arrange on 4 salad plates. Place cheese in center of plates, browned side up. Arrange croutons around cheese.

MAKES 4 SERVINGS

OVERLEAF: *Picnic Vegetable Salad (page 76) and Southwestern Chicken Terrine (page 33)*

GRILLED EGGPLANT SALAD
Wolfgang Puck, Spago

2 large tomatoes, peeled, seeded, and chopped
3 shallots, minced
2 tablespoons chopped fresh mint
Olive oil
3 tablespoons vinegar
Salt, freshly ground white pepper
1 teaspoon grated lemon peel
2 white eggplants
2 yellow tomatoes
16 mint leaves

Combine the chopped tomatoes, shallots, and chopped mint in a bowl. Add ⅓ cup olive oil and the vinegar. Season to taste with salt and pepper. Add lemon peel. Refrigerate at least 1 hour to blend flavors.

Cut the eggplants into ¼-inch slices. Sprinkle with salt and pepper, and brush both sides of each slice with olive oil. Place eggplant slices on grill over low coals and cook until eggplant is browned on both sides, brushing frequently with olive oil to keep moistened. Keep warm.

When ready to serve, cut the tomatoes into ¼-inch slices. Pour chopped tomato mixture on platter, spreading to cover bottom. Alternately, arrange overlapping slices of eggplant and tomato. Insert a mint leaf between each vegetable slice. Sprinkle with salt and pepper and a splash of olive oil if needed.

MAKES 6 SERVINGS

GRILLED RADICCHIO SALAD
Le St. Germain

4 whole small radicchio
Olive oil
Salt, white pepper
Watercress or parsley sprigs, for garnish

Rinse and dry radicchio. Brush the surface with olive oil. Season to taste with salt and pepper. Place on a grill over low coals and cook, turning often, until outer leaves are barely wilted. Serve garnished with watercress or parsley as an appetizer or salad course.

MAKES 4 SERVINGS

RADICCHIO AND BEAN SALAD
Rex Il Ristorante

½ pound brown beans (*fagioli borlotti*)
1 carrot
1 onion, peeled
1 stalk celery with leaves
2 tablespoons butter
2 tablespoons olive oil
2 rosemary sprigs, leaves only (discard stem)
¼ cup chopped parsley
4 sage leaves
2 cups torn radicchio
Virgin olive oil
Red wine vinegar
Salt, pepper

Soak the beans in water to cover overnight. Rinse and place in a saucepan with fresh water to cover. Add the carrot, onion, and celery, and bring to a boil. Reduce heat and simmer over low heat for 1 hour. Discard the carrot, onion, and celery.

Heat the butter and oil in a skillet. Add the rosemary, parsley, and sage and sauté 2 minutes. Add the beans and heat through. Place the radicchio on a platter. Season to taste with oil, vinegar, salt, and pepper. Toss. Top with the warm bean mixture.

MAKES 6 SERVINGS

WARM VEGETABLE SALAD WITH TRUFFLES
Patrick Terrail, Ma Maison

3 carrots
2 turnips
½ pound green beans
2 pounds tomatoes
Vinegar
1 celery heart
1 quart chicken broth
Butter
¼ pound snow peas
½ pound mâche
Radicchio
Vinaigrette (recipe follows)
1 ounce fresh truffles, cut in julienne strips

Peel and clean the carrots and turnips, trim the green beans, and peel the tomatoes. Place the prepared vegetables in water to cover with a few dashes of vinegar.

Cut the carrots, turnips, celery, and tomatoes in julienne strips, about 2 inches in length. Heat the chicken broth along with 1 tablespoon butter. Cook the vegetables separately in the broth, simmering 1 to 4 minutes until they are tender but firm, depending on their type and size. Cook the green beans and snow peas in boiling salted water until tender but crisp. Plunge in ice water to prevent cooking further, then drain.

Decorate a large platter with the mâche and radicchio. Then make an arrangement of the vegetables on the lettuces. Sprinkle with the vinaigrette, and garnish with truffles.

MAKES 8 SERVINGS

Vinaigrette

2 shallots, finely chopped
2 tablespoons chopped parsley
6 tablespoons vinegar
1/4 cup oil
Salt, pepper

Combine the shallots, parsley, vinegar, and oil in a bowl. Season to taste with salt and pepper.

PORTABLE PICNIC SPINACH SALAD
Susan Kranwinkle and Peggy Rahn, Inner Gourmet

2 cups torn spinach leaves
1/2 small red onion, thinly sliced
2 small oranges, sectioned
4 slices bacon, cooked and crumbled
1/2 cup chopped pecans
6 tablespoons oil
3 tablespoons cider vinegar
1/2 teaspoon Dijon mustard
1 clove garlic, peeled and halved
1/8 teaspoon dried basil
Salt, pepper, sugar

Place the spinach leaves, onion slices, and orange sections in separate plastic bags and chill well. Combine the crumbled bacon and pecans in a plastic bag and refrigerate. Beat together the oil, vinegar, and mustard until mixed. Add the garlic and basil and season to taste with salt, pepper, and sugar. Pour the dressing into a jar with a tight lid.

At serving time toss the spinach, onion, oranges, bacon, and pecans in a salad bowl. Remove the garlic from the dressing and discard. Shake dressing to blend and pour over spinach salad to coat well.

MAKES 3 TO 4 SERVINGS

SALADE MIKADO WITH TARRAGON VINAIGRETTE
Werner Albrecht, Five-Star Catering Co., Inc.

1 avocado, peeled and seeded
1/4 pound fresh shiitake mushrooms, thinly sliced
1/4 pound enoki mushrooms
1 tomato, peeled and cut into 8 wedges
8 radicchio leaves
Tarragon Vinaigrette (recipe follows)

Slice the avocado lengthwise into 16 slices. Arrange the avocado slices, shiitake slices, enoki mushrooms, tomato wedges, and radicchio attractively on 4 plates. Sprinkle 2 teaspoons tarragon vinaigrette over each serving.

MAKES 4 SERVINGS

Tarragon Vinaigrette

1/4 cup raspberry vinegar
1/4 cup olive oil
Salt, white pepper
1 tablespoon fresh tarragon leaves

Combine the raspberry vinegar, oil, and salt and white pepper to taste. Crush the tarragon leaves with a mortar and pestle. Add the crushed leaves to the vinaigrette and mix well.

ABOVE: *Warm Scallop Salad with Roasted Red Peppers (page 69)*

RIGHT: *Asperges aux Arrow-root Vinaigrette de Prune (page 68)*

OPPOSITE: *Trumps Seafood Salad (page 72)*

ASPERGES AUX ARROWROOT VINAIGRETTE DE PRUNE
(Asparagus in a Blanket with Plum Vinaigrette)
Susumu Fukui, La Petite Chaya

18 to 24 asparagus spears
2 tablespoons plus 1 teaspoon arrowroot starch
4 tablespoons puréed pickled Japanese red plum (see note)
1 tablespoon oil
Rice wine vinegar or lemon juice to taste
1 tablespoon sugar or to taste
Julienne strips of cucumber, for garnish
Very fine julienne strips of carrot, for garnish
Very fine julienne strips of daikon (Japanese radish), for
  garnish

Clean and cook the asparagus in a small amount of boiling water until tender but crisp, about 7 minutes, depending on thickness and size. Plunge into iced water to prevent further cooking.

Stir the arrowroot in 2 tablespoons water until dissolved. Pour into a large 11 x 17-inch baking sheet, tilting to completely cover the bottom with a film of the arrowroot. Place over a larger pan of hot water; set the stacked pans over 2 burners (or a griddle) set on a low heat. Cook until arrowroot layer solidifies, about 1 to 2 minutes. Submerge the sheet of arrowroot into the pan of hot water for a few seconds until the arrowroot layer becomes transparent. Drain off the hot water. Set aside the sheet of the clear, solidified arrowroot.

Combine the plum purée, oil, rice vinegar, and sugar to taste in a bowl. Stir to blend well. Arrange the asparagus on a platter. Cut the arrowroot gel large enough to cover all but the tips of the asparagus. Lift the gel carefully from the pan (place in cold water to keep from sticking if necessary), and place it on the asparagus, exposing only the tips. Sprinkle dressing over salad. Garnish with strips of cucumber, carrot, and daikon, forming into "S" shapes if possible.

MAKES 4 TO 6 SERVINGS

Note: If puréed pickled Japanese red plums are not available, soak canned, salted pickled plums in water overnight to remove any salt. Drain, and purée enough plums to make 4 tablespoons.

ITALIAN SALAD
Claudio Marchesan, Prego

2 medium zucchini, cut into finely shaved or julienne strips
Hearts of 1 bunch celery, cut into finely shaved or julienne
  strips
1/2 pound small beets, peeled and finely shaved or cut into
  julienne strips
4 paper-thin slices Parmesan cheese, cut into fine julienne
  strips
4 extra-thin slices prosciutto, cut into fine julienne strips
1/2 cup crumbled feta cheese
Balsamic Vinegar Dressing (recipe follows)

Among each of 4 plates, mound one-quarter of the zucchini on one side of the plate. Mound one-quarter of the celery on the other side. Then mound one-quarter of the beets, one-quarter of the Parmesan over the zucchini, one-quarter of the prosciutto over the celery, and one-quarter of crumbled feta cheese over the beets. Drizzle each plate with the balsamic vinegar dressing.

MAKES 4 SERVINGS

Balsamic Vinegar Dressing

1/3 cup balsamic vinegar
1/3 cup extra-virgin olive oil
Salt, pepper

Combine the vinegar and oil and season to taste with salt and pepper. Shake or stir vigorously.

GREEN BEAN NEST WITH SCALLOP EGGS
Janet Trefethen, Trefethen Vineyards

2 1/2 pounds small tender green beans, trimmed
1/2 cup unsalted butter
1 1/2 pounds bay scallops
1/3 cup mayonnaise
2/3 cup sour cream
1 teaspoon lemon juice, or to taste

1 tablespoon chopped green onions (green tops only)
Vinaigrette (recipe follows)
Finely chopped savory or parsley

Cook the beans in a large pot of boiling salted water until just crisp-tender. Drain. Place beans in cold water to stop cooking, drain, and refrigerate.

Melt the butter in a skillet over medium heat. Sauté scallops just until done, 1 to 2 minutes. Chill the scallops.

Just before serving, combine the mayonnaise, sour cream, lemon juice, and green onions. Toss the scallops in the mixture. Combine the beans with the vinaigrette. Arrange the beans in the form of a nest on a serving dish. Place scallops in center. Sprinkle with savory.

MAKES 8 SERVINGS

Vinaigrette

3/4 cup olive oil
1/4 cup sherry vinegar
Finely chopped fresh tarragon
Finely chopped fresh savory
Salt, pepper

Combine the oil, vinegar, tarragon, savory, and season to taste with salt and pepper. Shake well in a covered jar.

WARM SCALLOP SALAD WITH ROASTED RED PEPPERS
Gary Danko, Beringer Vineyards

1 cup fish broth
2 shallots, minced
1 cup sauvignon blanc
1/4 cup white wine vinegar or cider vinegar
1/2 teaspoon black pepper
Few strips peeled ginger root
1 to 2 teaspoons Dijon mustard
1/2 cup cold butter plus 2 tablespoons
1/4 cup walnut oil, approximately
1 1/2 pounds scallops, cleaned
6 bunches mâche or baby red leaf lettuce
1 small head radicchio
3 ripe avocados

3 large red peppers, roasted, peeled, and sliced
1/4 cup toasted walnut halves
Herb sprigs, for garnish (use any seasonal herbs)
Niçoise olives, for garnish

Combine the fish broth, shallots, sauvignon blanc, vinegar, pepper, and ginger in a skillet. Bring to a vigorous boil and boil until liquid is reduced to a glaze. Blend in the mustard. Gradually add the 1/2 cup butter, bit by bit, to form an emulsion. Add walnut oil to taste. Keep warm.

Heat 2 tablespoons butter in another skillet. Add the scallops. Sauté until opaque, about 3 to 4 minutes.

To assemble salad, place the lettuce and radicchio on 6 plates. Peel, pit, and slice avocados and fan out on the greens. Arrange the scallops and roasted peppers on plates. Sprinkle with walnuts. Garnish with sprigs of herbs and olives.

MAKES 8 SERVINGS

Note: Although mâche and radicchio are generally available from good produce purveyors, any colorful lettuces may be substituted.

PAPAYA WITH SHRIMP PIQUANT
Susan Kranwinkle and Peggy Rahn, Inner Gourmet

2 papayas, peeled, halved, and pitted
1 pound cooked bay shrimp
1 pomegranate
Bottled raspberry vinaigrette dressing
Danish cress (watercress may be substituted)

Cut the papaya halves lengthwise to make 8 pieces. Thinly slice each quarter lengthwise and arrange on salad plates. Place one-eighth of the cooked shrimp on each plate. Halve the pomegranate and remove the seeds. Sprinkle 2 tablespoons pomegranate seeds over each portion. Before serving, warm raspberry vinaigrette dressing in a small saucepan, then spoon it over the papaya and shrimp. Garnish with Danish cress.

MAKES 8 SERVINGS

Roy Yamaguchi
Grilled Prawn Salad (recipe at right)

GRILLED PRAWN SALAD
Roy Yamaguchi, 385 North

5 tablespoons olive oil
1 teaspoon chopped fresh thyme
½ teaspoon minced garlic
40 small prawns or 12 to 18 large prawns peeled and
    deveined
2 cups white wine
4 tablespoons unsalted butter
2 ounces sugar
12 cloves garlic
1 head radicchio
½ head escarole
1 cup mâche
6 ounces feta cheese, crumbled
1 tablespoon sherry wine vinegar
Salt, pepper
16 Niçoise olives

Prepare a hot grill. Combine 2 tablespoons olive oil, the thyme, and minced garlic in a small bowl. Dip the prawns in the oil mixture to coat well. Grill them over hot coals just until seared. Combine the white wine, butter, and sugar with the garlic cloves in a saucepan. Reduce to a syrupy consistency. (Garlic will be candied.) Set aside.

Combine the radicchio, escarole, and mâche in a bowl. Toss the greens with the garlic-syrup mixture (including the candied garlic) and the feta cheese. Add sherry vinegar, 3 tablespoons olive oil, and season to taste with salt and pepper. Distribute the greens among 6 plates. Arrange the prawns and olives over the greens.

MAKES 6 SERVINGS

ABALONE SALAD
Wolfgang Puck, Chinois on Main

2 small or 1 large head red leaf lettuce
1 bunch arugula or watercress
1 small head radicchio or red cabbage
12 fresh shiitake mushrooms
24 Chinese snow peas
4 fresh medium abalone (see note)
Juice of 2 or 3 limes
1 inch fresh ginger root, peeled and grated
Freshly ground pepper
1 tablespoon rice vinegar
2 tablespoons dark soy sauce
4 tablespoons extra-virgin olive oil
Salt, pepper
Lime or lemon wedges, for garnish, optional

Wash and dry the lettuce, arugula, and radicchio. Discard the mushroom stems and slice the tops in thin vertical slices. Rinse and dry the snow peas.

Remove the abalone from their shells, using the handle of a heavy spoon to break the muscle attachments. Reserve the shells. Clean the abalone well, discarding undesirable parts. Clean the shells thoroughly, dry, and set aside. Using a meat slicer, slice the abalone muscle crosswise into tissue-thin pieces. If the abalone can't be sliced tissue-thin, slice as thin as possible and pound each slice on a flat surface with a mallet or the flat end of a cleaver until tender and almost transparent but not shredded.

Combine the juice of 1 lime, 1 tablespoon grated ginger, and a grind or two of fresh pepper in a bowl. Add the abalone slices and toss to coat well. Marinate 15 to 20 minutes, stirring occasionally.

Combine the remaining lime juice, remaining ginger, vinegar, soy sauce, and 3 tablespoons olive oil in a small bowl. Tear the lettuce, arugula, and radicchio into coarse pieces and place in a large bowl; toss with the lime juice-olive oil dressing. Arrange the greens in the abalone shells or on serving plates. Set aside.

Heat the remaining 1 tablespoon olive oil in a skillet or sauté pan, add the mushrooms and peas, and season to taste with salt and pepper. Stir-fry briefly, just until the peas turn bright green. Remove from heat and toss to mix well. Pile hot mixture on top of greens in abalone shells. Top with the abalone slices. Garnish with lime or lemon wedges if desired.

MAKES 4 SERVINGS

Note: If abalone is not available, substitute sea scallops cut into paper-thin slices.

SNAPPER SALAD
Michael's

6 (3½-ounce) red snapper fillets
2 tablespoons butter, melted
½ pound baby zucchini
½ pound baby patty pan squash
18 baby green onions
¼ pound chanterelles

Arugula
Baby red leaf lettuce
Chervil sprigs
2 avocados
American black caviar
¼ yellow pepper, thinly sliced
¼ red pepper, thinly sliced
Cabernet Dressing (recipe follows)

Brush fish on both sides with butter. Place on a grill over medium coals and cook until tender. Do not overcook. Blanch the zucchini, patty pan squash, green onions, and chanterelles by separately adding to boiling salted water and simmering for 1 to 3 minutes, depending on type and size of vegetable. Drain and cool.

Arrange the zucchini, patty pan squash, green onions, chanterelles, arugula, red leaf lettuce (reserving 6 leaves for center), and chervil sprigs on 6 individual salad plates. Peel avocados and slice horizontally; arrange on each plate, slightly overlapping slices. Place a leaf of red lettuce in the center of each plate and over it place a grilled fish fillet. Dab each of the fish with about a heaping teaspoon of caviar. Crisscross with yellow and red pepper strips. Sprinkle with cabernet dressing.

MAKES 6 SERVINGS

Cabernet Dressing

¼ cup cabernet vinegar or sherry wine vinegar
¼ cup olive oil
Juice of 1 lime

Combine the vinegar, oil, and lime juice. Blend well.

MAKES ½ CUP

TRUMPS SEAFOOD SALAD FOR ONE
Michael Roberts, Trumps

½ cup lemon juice
Pinch ground cumin
Salt
1½ ounces cleaned squid
1 cup boiling water

1½ ounces scallops
1 jumbo shrimp
1 ounce salmon fillet
2 oysters, on the half shell (clams or mussels may be substituted)
Red Salsa (recipe follows)
Green Chile Salsa (recipe follows)
4 thin slices red onion
4 thin slices tomatillo
Chives
Lemon slice
Chopped cilantro or green onions

Combine the lemon juice, cumin, and salt in a cup. Place squid in boiling water to blanch for 15 seconds. Drain squid and place in a small bowl. Place the scallops, shrimp, and salmon in separate small bowls. Sprinkle lemon juice mixture over each fish, distributing evenly, and toss to coat well. Marinate, uncovered, 4 hours in the refrigerator.

Cover the bottom of a soup plate with 4 tablespoons red salsa. Arrange fish and oysters on shells on the plate, and spoon on 1 tablespoon green chile salsa. Decorate with fans of red onion and tomatillo, and chives. Garnish with a lemon slice twisted into an "S" shape. Sprinkle with chopped cilantro.

MAKES 1 SERVING

Red Salsa

6 tomatoes, cut up
½ to 1 red pepper, seeded and chopped
1 jalapeño chile, split and seeds removed
¼ bunch cilantro
½ onion, peeled and chopped
1 tablespoon olive oil
Salt, pepper

Combine the tomatoes, red pepper, jalapeño chile, cilantro, and onion in a blender or food processor. Using the chopping blade, process until coarsely chopped. Add olive oil and blend well. Season with salt and pepper to taste. Store in a well-covered container for up to a week or freeze for later use.

Green Chile Salsa

14 tomatillos, cut up
6 jalapeño chiles, split and seeds removed
⅛ red onion
½ bunch cilantro
Salt, pepper

Combine the tomatillos, jalapeños, onion, and cilantro in a blender or food processor. Using the chopping blade, process until coarsely chopped. Season to taste with salt and pepper. Store in a well-covered container for up to a week or freeze for later use.

Fiddlehead Fern and Smoked Chicken Salad

Michael Roberts, Trumps

¼ pound fiddlehead ferns
2 large ears fresh white or yellow corn, kernels removed
1 large red onion
1 red pepper, seeded and cut in strips
1 smoked chicken breast
Chicken Stock Dressing (recipe follows)

Cook the fiddleheads in a small amount of boiling salted water for 3 minutes. Drain and cool. Slice the fiddleheads horizontally and arrange the slices, overlapping slightly, on the sides of 6 salad plates. Place a heaping tablespoon of corn kernels in the center of each of the plates. Slice the onion vertically and arrange over the corn. Add the red pepper strips. Slice the chicken breast and arrange on plates. Serve with the chicken stock dressing.

MAKES 6 SERVINGS

Chicken Stock Dressing

2 cups chicken stock
2 ounces gumbo filé powder
1 egg yolk
¼ cup lemon juice
¼ cup olive oil
Salt, pepper

Place the chicken stock in a saucepan with gumbo filé powder. Cook until reduced to one-fifth of original quantity. Remove from heat. Beat the egg yolk with the lemon juice in a bowl. Add the chicken stock mixture, blending well. Stir in oil, and add salt and pepper to taste.

MAKES ABOUT 1¾ CUPS

Gyoza Duck Salad

Roy Yamaguchi, 385 North

6 uncooked gyozas (Japanese dumplings) (see note)
Olive oil
1 duck breast
2 teaspoons soy sauce
1 small clove garlic
1 inch orange peel
1 teaspoon grated ginger root
1 cup black and white chanterelles
1 head radicchio
1 Belgian endive
Chives
1 papaya
12 raspberries
½ cup crushed filberts
Escarole
Chicory
Basil
1 tablespoon raspberry vinegar
1 tablespoon walnut oil
Salt, white pepper to taste

Sauté the gyozas in 1 tablespoon oil in a large sauté pan. Add ⅓ cup water. Cover and steam; do not turn the gyozas. Drain the water, sprinkle the gyozas with oil, and cook until browned underneath. Set aside.

Place the duck breast in a shallow bowl. Add the soy sauce, garlic, orange peel, and ginger. Turn to mix well. Add the duck and the garlic mixture to the pan, cover, and steam-cook for about 20 minutes. Remove and set aside. Add 1 tablespoon olive oil to the pan. Add the chanterelles and sauté until barely tender, about 2 minutes. Remove from heat.

Place three radicchio leaves around a large serving platter. Arrange some endive around the platter. Garnish the center with chives. Slice the papaya in half, remove seeds, and slice crosswise. Fan out and place papaya "petals" on each side of the endive. Place the raspberries between the endive leaves.

OPPOSITE: *Szechuan Noodle Salad (page 76)*

ABOVE: *Composed California Corn Salad (page 77)*

Slice remaining radicchio and put in a large bowl. Add crushed filberts. Slice remaining endive into thin slices diagonally, and add to bowl. Slice the escarole, chicory, and basil, and add to the greens. Dress with the raspberry vinegar, oil, and salt and pepper. Toss to combine. Heap the salad in the center of the plate. Arrange the gyozas on each side of salad near the top. Slice the duck breast and arrange, star-fashion, on top of the salad.

MAKES 2 TO 4 SERVINGS

Note: Gyozas may be purchased from some Japanese restaurants or from stores that sell dumplings.

Szechuan Noodle Salad in Peanut Sauce
Hugh Carpenter

1 pound thin fettuccine or other noodles
2 tablespoons oil
1 cup julienned carrots
1 cup julienned green onions
¼ pound ham, cut into julienne strips
1 cup bean sprouts
1 cup julienned cucumber
1 cup julienned sweet red pepper
Peanut Sauce (recipe follows)

Cook fettuccine until tender. While noodles are still warm, toss with oil until well coated. Chill. Place the carrots in a sieve and pour boiling water over them. Immediately pat dry with paper towels, and chill. Wrap the green onions, ham, bean sprouts, cucumber, and red pepper separately, and chill until serving time. Bring noodles to room temperature before serving.

At serving time, place the noodles in the center of a large round bowl or platter. Arrange the vegetables and ham attractively in separate mounds around the edge. To serve, toss the noodles with the vegetables, ham, and peanut sauce.

MAKES 6 TO 8 SERVINGS

Note: The noodles and sauce must be at room temperature when tossed and served. If cold, the sauce will be too thick and will lose its creamy consistency.

Peanut Sauce

1½ tablespoons minced ginger root
1 tablespoon minced garlic
1 tablespoon minced green onion
6 tablespoons creamy peanut butter
2 tablespoons dark soy sauce
¼ cup red wine vinegar
1 tablespoon Chinese chili paste
1 teaspoon sugar
1 tablespoon sesame oil
2 tablespoons vegetable oil
1 tablespoon dry sherry
1 teaspoon Chinese-style hot, dry mustard
½ teaspoon salt
½ cup chicken stock

Combine the ginger, garlic, green onion, peanut butter, soy sauce, vinegar, chili paste, sugar, sesame and vegetable oils, sherry, dry mustard, salt, and chicken stock; blend thoroughly. Cover and set aside. Do not refrigerate. When ready to use, blend well again.

MAKES ABOUT 2½ CUPS

Picnic Vegetable Salad

6 small red potatoes
½ pound green beans, trimmed
1 cucumber, peeled
2 ears corn
18 cherry tomatoes, halved
Vinaigrette (recipe follows)
3 or 4 basil leaves, cut julienne

Peel the potatoes, leaving a ribbon of skin around the center. Cook in boiling salted water until tender. Cook green beans in boiling salted water until just tender-crisp, about 8 to 10 minutes. Cut the cucumber into strips. Cook the corn until tender. Plunge the beans and corn into cold water. Break each ear of corn into three sections. Cool vegetables. Combine the potatoes, green beans, corn, and cherry tomatoes in a bowl. Sprinkle with vinaigrette and carefully toss to coat vegetables. Chill. Sprinkle with basil.

MAKES 6 SERVINGS

Vinaigrette

¼ cup red wine vinegar
¼ cup walnut oil or olive oil
Salt, pepper

Combine the vinegar, walnut oil or olive oil, and season to taste with salt and pepper in a jar. Cover jar and shake well.

COMPOSED CALIFORNIA CORN SALAD

2 to 3 ears corn
1 small sweet red pepper, cut in strips
1 small green pepper, cut in strips
2 small yellow squash, sliced, or 1 yellow pepper, cut in wedges
2 small zucchini, sliced diagonally
2 small Japanese eggplants, cut in strips, optional
3 or 4 basil leaves, chopped
1 bunch arugula or bibb lettuce
1 bunch red leaf lettuce, sliced
½ cup rice wine vinegar
½ cup walnut oil, olive oil, or cottonseed oil
Salt, pepper

Cut the corn kernels from the cobs into a bowl. Set aside. Bring 2 quarts salted water to a rolling boil. Drop red and green pepper strips into the boiling water. Parboil for 1 minute or until color heightens. Remove peppers with a slotted spoon and drain. Refresh in a bowl of cold water. Set aside.

Add the yellow squash, zucchini, and eggplant to boiling water. Parboil 2 minutes. Remove with a slotted spoon and drain. Set aside.

Toss together the basil, arugula, and red leaf lettuce. Arrange greens on a large, shallow platter or tray. In a large bowl stir to combine the vinegar, walnut oil, and salt and pepper to taste. Add the corn kernels to the dressing, toss, and drain, reserving dressing. Arrange kernels in a spoke pattern to resemble sun rays over the greens, mounding some in the center. Separately add peppers, squash, zucchini, and eggplant to dressing, tossing lightly. Arrange red, green, and yellow vegetables in sections between corn kernel spokes. Pour any remaining dressing over salad.

MAKES 6 TO 8 SERVINGS

Note: In lieu of parboiling, vegetables may be sautéed in olive oil until crisp-tender, if desired.

AVOCADO CHEF SALAD

2 cups chopped red leaf or other lettuce
1 cup chopped watercress
½ cup thinly sliced mushrooms
½ cup pitted black olives
1 cup croutons
1 avocado, seeded, peeled, and cubed
2 hard-cooked eggs, sliced
4 ounces Swiss cheese, julienne-sliced
12 ounces cooked ham, turkey, and/or roast beef, julienne-sliced
Vinaigrette (recipe follows)

Combine the lettuce, watercress, mushrooms, olives, and croutons in a large bowl. Toss lightly to mix. Place the avocado and eggs on top of the salad. Top with Swiss cheese and meat. Just before serving, toss with dressing.

MAKES 6 SERVINGS

Vinaigrette

⅓ cup oil
¼ cup red wine vinegar
1 tablespoon capers, drained and chopped
¼ teaspoon salt
¼ teaspoon paprika
⅛ teaspoon garlic powder
⅛ teaspoon dry mustard

Combine the oil, vinegar, capers, salt, paprika, garlic powder, and mustard in a jar with a tight-fitting lid. Shake vigorously. Chill, covered, until ready to serve. Shake well before using.

HAWAIIAN CHICKEN SALAD

3 whole chicken breasts, skinned and boned
1½ cups sour cream
½ cup chutney, finely chopped
1 to 1½ teaspoons curry powder
¼ teaspoon ground ginger
¼ cup toasted shredded coconut
2 cantaloupes, small honeydew melons, or large papayas
4 cups shredded lettuce, optional

Place chicken on a steamer rack over 1 cup boiling water. Cover and steam for 15 minutes or until cooked through, but still moist. Dice or shred the meat. Combine the sour cream, chutney, curry powder, and ginger until mixed. Mix the dressing with the chicken and coconut. Chill.

Cut the cantaloupes, honeydew melons, or papayas in halves, remove seeds, and fill the cavities with the chicken salad. Or, spoon the chicken salad on shredded lettuce and garnish with slices of the fruit. If desired, cover salad with dressing, and arrange slices of melon on top to form a crown. Sprinkle with coconut.

MAKES 6 SERVINGS

MAI FUN CHICKEN SALAD

Napa cabbage or Savoy cabbage leaves
2 cups mai fun (Chinese rice sticks), prepared according to
    package directions
1 cup finely shredded carrots
2 large cooked chicken breasts, skinned, boned, and cut
    into thin slices
½ cup sugar snap peas, blanched and chilled
Vegetable garnishes (slices of Japanese or regular cucumber,
    straw mushrooms, carrot flowers)
Hoisin Dressing (recipe follows)

For each serving, line a plate with cabbage leaves, and over them arrange a layer of mai fun. Then arrange the shredded carrots, chicken slices, sugar snap peas, and vegetable garnish on the plates as desired. Pass the dressing with the salad.

MAKES 2 SERVINGS

HOISIN DRESSING

3 tablespoons rice vinegar or white wine vinegar
¼ cup salad oil
1 tablespoon hoisin sauce
2 teaspoons sesame seeds
2 teaspoons minced fresh ginger root

Combine the vinegar, oil, hoisin sauce, sesame seeds, and ginger root in a jar with a lid. Cover and shake well. Chill. Shake again before serving.

SPANISH CHICKEN SALAD

3½ cups cooked chicken strips
1 small crisp head lettuce, shredded
1 large red onion, thinly sliced
½ cup olive oil
¼ cup red wine vinegar
Salt, pepper
Lettuce leaves
2 oranges, peeled and sliced, for garnish
2 avocados, peeled and sliced, for garnish
1 bunch small radishes, trimmed and sliced, for garnish

Place the chicken, lettuce, and onion in a bowl. Thoroughly combine the oil and vinegar. Season to taste with salt and pepper. Pour over the salad, toss gently, then arrange the chicken on lettuce leaves. Garnish with orange, avocado, and radish slices.

MAKES 6 SERVINGS

CLOCKWISE FROM RIGHT: *Spanish Chicken Salad; Mai Fun Chicken Salad; Hawaiian Chicken Salad (recipes at left)*

Pasta, Pizza, Rice, and Eggs

Pasta Pesto
Boh!

Corkscrew Macaroni with Spinach Pesto
Tutto Italia

Rex's Farfalle
Rex Il Ristorante

Pasta with Szechuan Spiced Shrimp
Bob Brody, Sheraton Harbor Island West, San Diego

Tagliarini Verde al Capra
Pasta Etc.

Pasta Salad with Three Bell Peppers
Ken Frank, La Toque

Calzone
Alice Waters, Chez Panisse, Berkeley

The Leopard's Dish
(Timballo di Pasta alla Siciliana)
Celestino Drago, Celestino Ristorante

Pad Thai
Chan Dara Siamese Kitchen

Pizza Rustica
Sorrento Italian Market

Risotto Milanese
Ueli Huegli, Adriano's Ristorante

Eggs with Salmon and Sorrel Sauce
Wolfgang Puck

Eggs in Jelly
Liz Martini, Louis M. Martini Winery

Spinach Cannelloni

Wagon Wheel Pasta Salad

Confetti Penne

Walnut Pasta Salad

Pasta with Chicken and Almonds

Athenian Pizza

Saffron Rice

Imagination runs rampant when chefs invent new recipes for such basic ingredients as pastas, rice, and eggs. And nowhere do the various ethnic influences mix and interplay as they do with these foods.

Pasta with Szechuan Spiced Shrimp (page 81), created by Bob Brody of the Sheraton Harbor Island West in San Diego, crosses Italian pasta with shrimp and spicy Chinese seasonings.

Alice Waters has used the marvelous goat cheeses of nearby Sonoma Valley to make an herb-scented pizza with a difference. Her Calzone (page 84) is a delectable crisp pocket of dough filled with melted goat cheeses.

In this section, too, you will find a recipe from another great California chef, Wolfgang Puck. His Eggs with Salmon and Sorrel Sauce (page 88) can be made with either fresh or smoked salmon, and is a dish that rewards very small efforts with spectacularly good flavor.

Thailand, France, Italy, and the United States have influenced these foods, happy products of California's ethnic diversity.

PASTA PESTO
Boh!

2 tablespoons toasted pine nuts
1/4 pound basil, scant
1 large spinach leaf
6 cloves garlic
1/3 cup freshly grated Pecorino Romano cheese
1/3 cup Parmesan cheese
1 cup olive oil
1 pound linguine, fresh or dried

Combine the nuts, basil, spinach, and garlic in a food processor. Add cheeses and oil, and mix.

Cook the linguine in boiling salted water to cover until linguine is al dente. Pour sauce over pasta. Toss to mix well.

MAKES 4 TO 6 SERVINGS

CORKSCREW MACARONI WITH SPINACH PESTO
Tutto Italia

1 pound corkscrew macaroni
Olive oil
1/2 cup mayonnaise
Spinach Pesto (recipe follows)
Pine nuts, for garnish
Diced pimiento, for garnish

Cook the macaroni in boiling water seasoned with 1 tablespoon salt and 1 tablespoon olive oil until tender but firm, about 9 minutes. Drain in a colander, then transfer to a large bowl. Add mayonnaise and 2 tablespoons olive oil. Mix well. Blend in the spinach pesto. Chill. Garnish with pine nuts and diced pimiento.

MAKES 8 TO 12 SERVINGS

Spinach Pesto

1 bunch spinach, trimmed
4 cloves garlic
Salt, pepper
1/2 cup olive oil

Place the spinach, garlic, and salt and pepper to taste in a food processor. Gradually add the oil in a thin stream through the feed tube and blend until the sauce is the consistency of thin mayonnaise.

REX'S FARFALLE
Rex Il Ristorante

2 quarts lamb stock (see note)
1 ounce beet-flavored butterfly pasta (see note)
2 ounces spinach-flavored butterfly pasta
2 ounces black (squid ink) butterfly pasta
2 ounces egg butterfly pasta
1/2 cup butter
1/3 cup grated Parmesan cheese

Bring the lamb stock to a boil, reserving 1/2 cup. Add all of the pasta, and cook until pasta is just tender to the bite. Drain.

Melt the butter in a skillet. Add reserved 1/2 cup stock and simmer over high heat until broth is slightly reduced. Mix in the cheese until blended. Pour over pasta. Mix lightly.

MAKES 4 SERVINGS

Note: Beef, or chicken stock or water may be substituted for lamb stock for cooking the pasta. Any broth may be used for preparing the sauce.

Any pasta of different flavors may be used if beet, spinach, or black pasta is unavailable.

PASTA WITH SZECHUAN SPICED SHRIMP
Bob Brody, Sheraton Harbor Island West, San Diego

1/4 pound spinach leaves
2 tomatoes
16 large shrimp

TOP: *Tagliarini Verde al Capra (page 84)*

RIGHT: *Spinach Cannelloni (page 89); Pimiento-Wrapped Italian Sausage (page 137); Artichoke Vinaigrette (page 45); Corkscrew Macaroni with Spinach Pesto (page 81)*

2 tablespoons olive oil
2 cloves garlic
¼ cup Chinese chili paste (see note)
1 pound colored dry or fresh penne, fettuccine, or other pasta
½ cup butter, cut into 10 pieces

Wash spinach and remove stems. Peel and seed tomatoes. Chop roughly. Clean and devein shrimp. Set aside.

Heat the olive oil in a skillet. Add garlic. Sauté a few seconds. Add the shrimp and the chili paste. Cook until the shrimp turns pink. Set aside.

Meanwhile, cook the pasta in a pot of boiling water. Drain and arrange the pasta on a serving platter or individual plates. Arrange the shrimp over the pasta. Place the tomatoes and spinach in a medium skillet. Sauté the vegetables in half the butter until tender. Then add remaining butter, bit by bit, until all the butter in pan is melted. Pour equal amounts of spinach-tomato-butter mixture over the pasta.

MAKES 4 SERVINGS

Note: Chili paste is available at any Chinese market. If not available, mix together 2 tablespoons red chili powder, 2 cloves garlic, mashed, and ½ cup rice wine vinegar. Store marinade in the refrigerator to use as needed.

Tagliarini Verde al Capra
Pasta Etc.

1 pound fresh spinach tagliarini or fettuccine
½ cup oil and vinegar dressing
Salt, pepper
4 ounces goat cheese, crumbled
1 package enoki mushrooms, stems trimmed

Cook the tagliarini in boiling salted water until tender, but still firm. Drain and cool. Season with dressing and salt and pepper. Crumble the cheese and toss with the seasoned pasta. Surround the pasta with a wall of enoki mushrooms.

MAKES 4 TO 6 SERVINGS

Pasta Salad with Three Bell Peppers
Ken Frank, La Toque

1 pound fettuccine
1 green pepper
1 red pepper
1 yellow pepper
3 sun-dried tomatoes, cut in julienne strips
2 tablespoons fresh Syrian or other basil
¼ cup olive oil, preferably reserved from a jar of sun-dried tomatoes
Sherry wine vinegar
Salt, pepper

Cook the fettuccine in generously salted boiling water until barely tender. Drain. While fettuccine cooks, roast the peppers on a grill or under a broiler until the skins blister. Plunge in ice water. Peel off skins. Slice peppers into julienne strips. Add peppers and tomato strips to the pasta in a large bowl. Toss with olive oil and a splash of vinegar. Season to taste with salt and pepper. Let stand about 2 hours in refrigerator to blend flavors.

MAKES 6 SERVINGS

Calzone
Alice Waters, Chez Panisse, Berkeley

2 ounces Sonoma goat cheese (or other kind of goat cheese), crumbled
2 pounds French goat cheese such as Boucheron, crumbled
7 ounces mozzarella cheese, grated
2 slices prosciutto, julienned
2 tablespoons finely cut fresh chives
2 tablespoons minced fresh parsley
1 thyme sprig, chopped
1 marjoram sprig, chopped
2 small cloves garlic, minced
Black pepper
Pizza Dough (recipe follows)

Combine the goat cheeses, mozzarella, prosciutto, chives, parsley, thyme, marjoram, and garlic in a large bowl. Add pepper to taste and mix well.

Roll out the pizza dough to a circle about 14 inches in diameter or divide dough into 2 or 3 pieces to make small calzone. For 1 large calzone, place the entire filling on half of the dough, leaving a 1-inch margin around the edges.

Moisten the edges with water and fold over the other dough half to make the edges meet. Fold up the edges to form a sort of running curl, pinching to seal tightly. Place on a floured paddle and slide onto the oven floor. For smaller calzone, use the same method, adjusting the amount of filling as needed. Bake at 450 to 500 degrees for 15 to 25 minutes, or until bottom of calzone is crisp. For small calzone, reduce the cooking time by half.

MAKES 1 LARGE CALZONE

Pizza Dough

2 teaspoons dry yeast
1/4 cup rye flour
1 tablespoon milk
2 tablespoons olive oil
1/2 teaspoon salt
1 3/4 cups unbleached all-purpose flour

Make a sponge by mixing together 1/4 cup lukewarm water, yeast, and rye flour in a bowl. Let rise 20 to 30 minutes. Then add 1/2 cup lukewarm water, the milk, olive oil, salt, and all-purpose flour. Mix the dough with a wooden spoon, then turn out onto a floured board and knead until soft and slightly sticky. Use quick, light motions with your hands to prevent dough from sticking. Add more flour to board as you knead the dough, but no more than is absolutely necessary. Knead 10 to 15 minutes until dough is soft and elastic.

Place the dough in a bowl that has been brushed with olive oil. Oil the surface of the dough to prevent a crust from forming. Cover the bowl with a clean towel and place in a warm place, about 90 to 110 degrees, to rise. (An oven heated just by a pilot light is a good spot.) Let dough rise 40 minutes longer. Shape as desired.

THE LEOPARD'S DISH
(*Timballo di Pasta alla Siciliana*)
Celestino Drago, Celestino Ristorante

1 1/2 pounds penne
Ragout (recipe page 87)
Béchamel Sauce (recipe page 87)
1/4 cup butter
10 chicken livers
Pie Pastry (recipe page 87)
1/2 pound prosciutto, thinly sliced
4 hard-cooked eggs, cut into eighths
1/2 pound water-packed mozzarella cheese, sliced
1 medium truffle, thinly sliced
Cinnamon
4 or 5 fresh or dried bay leaves
1 egg yolk, beaten

Cook penne in vigorously boiling salted water until al dente or firm to the bite. Drain. Stir in the ragout and béchamel sauce, then set aside.

Melt butter in a skillet. Add the chicken livers and sauté until browned but pink inside. Cool, slice, and set aside.

Divide the pastry in half, reserving extra for cutouts. Roll out half the pastry to 18 inches or large enough to line a 12-inch bowl. Alternately layer the macaroni mixture, chicken livers, prosciutto slices, hard-cooked egg wedges, mozzarella, and truffle slices in pan, sprinkling occasionally with cinnamon and topping each layer with one or two bay leaves, until all the ingredients are used.

Roll out other pastry half and fit over the filling. Trim edges and seal, brushing the rim with egg yolk. Invert onto a large, well greased pizza pan or large baking sheet.

Roll out remaining pastry. Using small and large cutters make desired decorative shapes such as small diamonds and flowers, as well as six 2-inch circles, which should be loosely folded in half. Brush pastry dome with egg yolk. Fasten cutouts to dome, using arches for base, and circle halves as crown. Fasten small cutouts all around the dome. Brush again with egg yolk and bake at 350 degrees for 45 minutes or until pastry is golden. Let stand 10 minutes, then transfer to serving platter. Garnish as desired. To serve, break crust and spoon out some of the pasta with crust for each serving, or cut into wedges. Be sure to discard the bay leaves.

MAKES 10 TO 12 SERVINGS

Ragout

½ cup oil
1 small onion, peeled and chopped
2 carrots, diced
2 stalks celery, chopped
1 clove garlic, minced
1 teaspoon chopped fresh rosemary
1 teaspoon chopped fresh sage
1 pound ground beef
1 pound ground veal
Salt, pepper
Pinch nutmeg
1 cup dry red wine
2 pounds tomatoes (about 8), peeled, seeded, and chopped
　or 1 (1-pound) can whole peeled tomatoes, drained and
　chopped
2 chicken breasts, skinned, boned, and diced

Heat ¼ cup of the oil in a large skillet. Add the onion, carrots, celery, garlic, rosemary, and sage. Sauté until onion is tender. Add the beef and veal and sauté until meat is browned and crumbly. Add salt, pepper, and nutmeg to taste. Stir in the wine. Bring to a boil, reduce heat, and simmer until reduced by half. Add tomatoes and simmer 45 minutes or until thickened.

In a separate pan, heat remaining ¼ cup oil. Sauté the diced chicken breasts until tender and golden brown. Add to the ragout.

Béchamel Sauce

½ cup butter
¼ cup flour
1 quart milk, scalded
Salt, pepper
Pinch nutmeg

Melt the butter in a large saucepan. Stir in the flour until smooth. Gradually stir in milk, salt, pepper, and nutmeg. Cook and stir until slightly thickened.

The Leopard's Dish (page 85)

Pie Pastry

6 cups flour
1 teaspoon salt
1 pound plus 8 ounces butter, softened
6 medium eggs

Mix flour with salt. Make a well in the center of the flour mixture. Into it add the butter by bits and the eggs. Gradually work the flour into eggs and butter until a soft dough is formed. Do not overwork dough. Chill until ready to use.

PAD THAI
Chan Dara Siamese Kitchen

1 pound pad thai (vermicelli noodles)
¼ cup bottled fish sauce
2 tablespoons sugar
½ cup tamarind juice
6 tablespoons vinegar
1 teaspoon chopped California chiles
Oil
¼ pound lean pork, thinly sliced to 1 x 2-inch pieces
4 to 6 medium to large shrimp, shelled and deveined
1 tablespoon dried shrimp
2 tablespoons diced baked soybean cake
2 eggs
1 tablespoon crushed peanuts
Bean sprouts
2 green onions, finely sliced

Soak the noodles in water to cover. Combine the fish sauce, sugar, tamarind juice, vinegar, and chiles in a bowl. Heat 3 tablespoons oil in a medium skillet. Add the pork, shrimp, dried shrimp, soybean cake, and fish sauce mixture, and cook over high heat until pork is browned and well cooked.

Thoroughly drain the noodles and add to the skillet. Stir just enough to dry slightly. Push noodle mixture to one side of skillet. Add 1 tablespoon oil to skillet and heat. Add eggs and scramble until firm. Top eggs with noodle mixture, 2 teaspoons crushed peanuts and 2 cups bean sprouts. Serve topped with additional bean sprouts, green onion, and remaining teaspoon peanuts.

MAKES 2 TO 4 SERVINGS

Note: Noodles, soybean cake, dried shrimp, tamarind juice or paste, and fish sauce can be found in most Oriental markets.

PIZZA RUSTICA
Sorrento Italian Market

3 cups flour
1 tablespoon baking powder
Pinch salt
3/4 cup butter, softened
4 eggs
Mixed Cheese Filling (recipe follows)

Sift together the flour, baking powder, and salt into a large bowl. Work in butter as for pastry. Stir in 3 eggs just until mixed. Do not overmix or dough will become tough. Set aside.

Prepare cheese filling. Divide the dough in half. Roll out 1 portion to fit a greased 12-inch pizza pan, bringing up edges to form rim. Pour mixed cheese filling into the pie shell.

Roll out remaining dough to fit over filling, reserving a small portion of dough to decorate the top of the pie. Seal edges. Roll out small piece of reserved dough and cut into floral or geometric shapes. Beat remaining egg in a small bowl. Brush beaten egg over pastry. Arrange pastry cutouts over pie dough. Brush cutouts with egg wash. Bake at 350 degrees for 45 to 50 minutes or until golden brown.

MAKES 8 TO 10 SERVINGS

Mixed Cheese Filling

1 1/4 cups ricotta cheese
1 (1-pound) package tuma cheese, diced (see note)
6 ounces mozzarella cheese, diced
1/3 pound grated Pecorino or Romano cheese
5 eggs, lightly beaten
1/4 pound diced dry Italian salami (soppressata)
1/4 pound diced prosciutto
2 links fresh Italian sausage
Pinch chopped fresh parsley
Pinch oregano
Pinch chopped sweet basil
2 cloves garlic, minced
Pinch pepper

Combine the ricotta, tuma, mozzarella, and Pecorino cheeses. In a large bowl, mix the eggs, salami, prosciutto, sausage, parsley, oregano, basil, garlic, and pepper. Blend in the cheese mixture.

Note: Tuma cheese is a semisoft cheese often available in Middle Eastern as well as Italian grocery stores. Mexican panela cheese may be substituted.

RISOTTO MILANESE
Ueli Huegli, Adriano's Ristorante

1/2 cup butter or margarine
1 shallot or large onion, chopped
2 cups imported Italian rice (Arborio or Vialone)
1 quart chicken broth or half chicken broth and half white wine
1/2 teaspoon saffron threads, optional
Salt to taste
Pinch pepper
1/2 cup grated Parmesan cheese

Melt half the butter in a large shallow saucepan. Add the shallot and sauté until tender. Add the rice and sauté until glazed. Mix 1/4 cup broth with the saffron, if using. Add to rice. Simmer, stirring constantly, until liquid is absorbed. Add 1/2 cup more broth, season with salt and pepper. Simmer, stirring constantly until liquid is absorbed. Continue to add broth by half-cupfuls and cook until each addition is absorbed. Continue stirring constantly until the rice is creamy, and broth is used up. Stir in the cheese and remaining butter. Stir until butter melts. Serve at once.

MAKES 8 SERVINGS

EGGS WITH SALMON AND SORREL SAUCE
Wolfgang Puck

Butter
1/2 pound sliced fresh salmon or thinly sliced smoked salmon
1 1/2 cups heavy cream
12 sorrel leaves, stems removed
Freshly ground black pepper
4 eggs

Butter four 2 1/2-inch ramekins with 1 teaspoon butter each. Chill 15 minutes. Line the bottom of the ramekins with a salmon slice and 1 tablespoon cream each. Chill again until ready to use.

Cut the sorrel into 1/4-inch-thick strips. Heat 1 tablespoon butter in saucepan and add the sorrel. Sauté 1 minute. Add remaining cream. Reduce by half. Season to taste with black pepper and keep warm.

Break 1 egg into each ramekin. Bake at 350 degrees for 20 minutes or until egg whites are firm but still soft. Serve with sorrel sauce.

MAKES 4 SERVINGS

Eggs in Jelly
Liz Martini, Louis M. Martini Winery

1 envelope unflavored gelatin
1/2 cup sweet sherry
1 (10 1/2-ounce) can beef consommé
1/2 cup dry white wine
Small gherkins or pimiento-stuffed olives
6 small or medium hard-cooked eggs, cut in half lengthwise
1/2 to 1 (4 1/2-ounce) can liver pâté
Mayonnaise, or *Lemon Juice and Olive Oil Dressing* (recipe follows)

Soften the gelatin in 1/4 cup cold water. Combine the sherry and 1/2 cup water in a small saucepan. Bring to a boil. Boil 2 to 3 minutes, then add the softened gelatin, consommé, and white wine.

Cover the bottom of an oiled 9-inch-square decorative baking dish with 1/2 of the gelatin mixture. Chill until set. Evenly space 12 gherkins in dish. Top with egg halves, cut side down. Slice the pâté and cut into any desired geometric or floral design using aspic cutters or a knife. Arrange around the eggs. Cover with remaining gelatin mixture. Cover and refrigerate until set. Serve with mayonnaise, or with the lemon juice and olive oil dressing, if desired.

MAKES 6 SERVINGS

Lemon Juice and Olive Oil Dressing

1/4 cup lemon juice
1/2 teaspoon salt
1/4 teaspoon coarsely ground black pepper
1/2 teaspoon dried tarragon
1/4 teaspoon garlic salt
1/2 teaspoon prepared mustard
3/4 cup olive oil

Combine the lemon juice, salt, pepper, tarragon, garlic salt, mustard, and olive oil. Shake well.

Note: For indioidual jellied molds, use custard cups for each egg half, placing egg halves cut side down, and decorating with pâté and gherkins. Unmold when set.

Spinach Cannelloni

10 spinach lasagne noodles
1 pound spinach, stems removed, or 2 (10-ounce) packages frozen chopped spinach, thawed and squeezed dry
1 1/4 cups butter
1 pound boneless chicken breasts, diced
1/2 pound grated Parmesan cheese
3 to 4 tablespoons half and half
1/8 teaspoon nutmeg
Salt, pepper
Marinara Sauce (recipe follows)

Cook the lasagne noodles in boiling salted water until tender; drain. Rinse in cold water and drain again. Sauté the spinach in 1/4 cup butter until tender. Set aside. Heat another 1/4 cup butter and sauté the chicken until golden. Combine the chicken and spinach. Melt remaining 3/4 cup butter in a small saucepan. Stir in the Parmesan cheese, then stir in enough half and half to form a smooth cream-like sauce. Add nutmeg and season to taste with salt and pepper. Pour the sauce over the chicken mixture, stirring until blended. Fill the lasagne noodles with the chicken mixture and roll up. Arrange in a 13 x 9-inch baking pan. Spoon over the marinara sauce. Bake at 375 degrees for 20 to 30 minutes or until hot and bubbly.

MAKES 10 CANNELLONI

Marinara Sauce

1 cup chopped onion
1 clove garlic, minced
2 tablespoons olive oil
1/4 teaspoon basil
1/4 teaspoon oregano
2 (1-pound, 12-ounce) cans whole tomatoes, drained and crushed
Salt, pepper

Sauté the onion and garlic in olive oil until tender. Stir in the basil and oregano. Add the tomatoes and season to taste with salt and pepper. Bring to a boil. Reduce heat, cover, and simmer for 30 minutes, stirring occasionally. Purée the sauce.

MAKES 3 CUPS

ABOVE: *Eggs with Salmon and Sorrel Sauce (page 88)*

LEFT: *Fresh thyme*

RIGHT: *Pasta with Chicken and Almonds; Walnut Pasta Salad; Confetti Penne (all recipes page 92)*

WAGON WHEEL PASTA SALAD

1 pound wagon wheel pasta or other type of pasta
2 tablespoons olive oil
1 green pepper, sliced
1 red pepper, sliced
1/2 to 2/3 cup chopped fresh dill
Vinaigrette Dressing (recipe follows)

Cook the pasta in boiling salted water until al dente. Drain and cool. Place in a large bowl.

Heat the oil in a skillet. Add the green and red peppers and sauté until barely tender. Add to the pasta along with the dill. Add vinaigrette. Toss to coat pasta well. Chill, covered, until serving time.

MAKES 8 SERVINGS

Vinaigrette Dressing

1 cup oil
1/3 cup red wine vinegar
1 tablespoon Dijon mustard
2 cloves garlic, crushed
Juice of 1 lemon
Salt and pepper to taste

Combine the oil, vinegar, mustard, garlic, lemon juice, and salt and pepper.

MAKES 1 1/2 CUPS

CONFETTI PENNE

1/2 pound penne or other tubular pasta
1 tablespoon oil
2 small carrots, peeled and cut into julienne slices
2 small zucchini, trimmed and cut into julienne slices
3 green onions, cut into julienne slices (including green tops)
2 tablespoons chopped basil leaves
1/4 cup heavy cream, whipped
2 tablespoons rice or cider vinegar
Salt, freshly ground black pepper
1/2 teaspoon sesame oil
Radicchio, fresh basil, baby zucchini, optional

Cook the penne in boiling salted water until al dente. Drain well. Toss with 1 tablespoon oil and chill, covered. Cook carrots just until tender-crisp. Chill.

At serving time, toss the penne with carrots, zucchini, green onions, basil, whipped cream, and vinegar. Season with salt and pepper. Stir in the sesame oil. Garnish with radicchio, fresh basil leaves, and baby zucchini, if desired.

MAKES 6 SERVINGS

WALNUT PASTA SALAD

1/2 pound red, green, and white spiral noodles
1 tablespoon walnut oil
3 ounces blue cheese
1/4 cup milk
1/2 cup sour cream
1/2 teaspoon garlic salt, optional
1 teaspoon lemon juice
1/4 to 1/2 cup chopped walnuts
Salt, freshly ground pepper
Belgian endive, watercress, optional

Cook noodles in boiling salted water until al dente. Drain well. Toss with walnut oil. Cover and chill.

Combine the cheese, milk, and sour cream in a blender until creamy. Stir in garlic salt, if using, and lemon juice. Toss with the noodles. Add walnuts and toss again. Season to taste with salt and pepper. Mound on a large serving platter or individual salad plates, and garnish with Belgian endive and watercress, if desired.

MAKES 4 TO 6 SERVINGS

PASTA WITH CHICKEN AND ALMONDS

1/2 pound carrot shell pasta
3 tablespoons olive oil
1/4 pound snow peas, trimmed
2 cups shredded or cubed cooked chicken, chilled
1 cup diagonally sliced celery
2 tablespoons balsamic vinegar
2 cloves garlic, pressed
1/2 teaspoon sugar

Salt, white pepper
½ cup slivered almonds, toasted
Lettuce leaves, optional

Cook pasta in boiling salted water until al dente. Drain well. Toss with 1 tablespoon olive oil and chill, covered. Blanch the snow peas in boiling salted water for 1 minute, or just until they turn bright green. Quickly drain and refresh in cold water. Drain.

Combine the pasta with the chicken, snow peas, and celery. Toss with remaining 2 tablespoons olive oil, vinegar, garlic, and sugar, and season to taste with salt and white pepper. Sprinkle with almonds. Serve on lettuce leaves, if desired.

MAKES 6 SERVINGS

ATHENIAN PIZZA

3 tablespoons oil
12 thin slices eggplant, diced
1 large red pepper, diced
6 pita breads
1½ cups prepared spaghetti sauce
2½ ounces pepperoni, sliced
1 small onion, thinly sliced

Heat 2 tablespoons oil in a large skillet over medium heat. Add the diced eggplant, a little at a time, and cook until golden brown, adding remaining oil as needed. Drain the eggplant on paper towels. Add the red pepper and cook until tender-crisp. Drain on paper towels.

Separate the pita breads, pulling completely apart into halves. Arrange on a baking sheet, cut sides up. Spread 2 tablespoons spaghetti sauce on each pita bread half. Top with some of the eggplant, red pepper, pepperoni, and onion slices. Bake at 400 degrees for 5 minutes.

MAKES 6 SERVINGS

SAFFRON RICE

2 tablespoons butter or margarine
Pinch saffron threads
2 cups rice
Salt, white pepper
5 cups boiling water

In a large saucepan melt the butter. Add the saffron and dissolve. Stir in the rice over low heat until rice becomes shiny. Stir in the salt and pepper and the boiling water. Heat to a simmer, stirring to prevent sticking. Cover and simmer over low heat until water is completely absorbed and rice is fluffy, about 30 minutes. Cover and set aside off heat until ready to serve.

MAKES 6 TO 8 SERVINGS

Fish and Shellfish

TOURNEDOS DE SAUMON
Laurent Quenioux, Seventh Street Bistro

SALMON IN RASPBERRY VINAIGRETTE
Werner Albrecht, Five-Star Catering Co., Inc.

TERRINE OF SALMON, CORN, AND JALAPEÑOS
John Sedlar, St. Estèphe

PAUPIETTE DE DOVER SOLE OLYMPIAD
Michel Blanchet, L'Ermitage

PAUPIETTE DE DORADE ROUGE
Susumu Fukui, La Petite Chaya

GRILLED TUNA SALAD
Ken Frank, La Toque

TUNA WITH TANGERINE-BUTTER SAUCE
Joe Venezia, Hotel Bel-Air

ROASTED SEA BASS WITH CRUST OF HERBS
Bruno Cirino, Antoine, Hotel Meridien, Newport
   Beach

SCAMPI MARE NOSTRUM
La Scala

SHRIMP WITH GREEN PEPPERCORN SAUCE
Joe Allen

SAUTÉ OF SQUID, SHRIMP, AND EGGPLANT
Bob Brody, Sheraton Harbor Island West, San Diego

SCALLOPS WITH LIME BUTTER
The First Street Bar and Grill, Claremont

STUFFED SCALLOP SURPRISE WITH SAFFRON SAUCE
Patrick Healy, Colette, Beverly Pavilion Hotel

LOBSTER WITH WILD WATERCRESS DRESSING
Joe Venezia, Hotel Bel-Air

STIR-FRIED OYSTERS WITH GARLIC AND
   GREEN ONIONS
Mon Kee Restaurant

CORN MOUSSE WITH CLAMS
(Mousse de Maïs aux Palourdes)
Joachim Splichal, Max au Triangle

POACHED CHILLED SALMON

GRILLED SALMON FILLETS IN LETTUCE

BAKED CATFISH FILLETS WITH HORSERADISH SAUCE

HUNAN-STYLE STEAMED FISH
(To Sze Tsen Yui)

FILLET MOSAIC WITH RED PEPPER SAUCE

CALIFORNIA BOUILLABAISSE

CRACKED CRAB NORTH BEACH

RED SNAPPER CHINOIS

Fish has become the preferred "meat" course for those concerned about cholesterol and fat in their diet. As a result, restaurants specializing in seafood are on the increase, but happily for Californians, our local catch comes from a long Pacific coastline stretching from Alaska to Baja, California and the variety of delicious fish and crustaceans native to these waters gives our menus a distinctive character and quality.

The new fish farming industry has brought us a steady supply of oysters from Drake's Bay, shrimp from solar aquacells in Sun City, catfish farmed in Sacramento (see the Baked Catfish Fillets with Horseradish Sauce, page 109), and salmon spawned in Bremerton, Washington, and transferred to saltwater ponds in Puget Sound (see Grilled Salmon Fillets in Lettuce, page 108).

From the sea there are such ethereal dishes as the Fillet Mosaic with Red Pepper Sauce (page 112), woven strips of salmon, sole, and spinach, a Sante Fe interpretation of French nouvelle cuisine given its local fame by John Sedlar of St. Estèphe restaurant in Manhattan Beach. There is even a rich and hearty California Bouillabaisse (page 112) that includes our own incomparable Dungeness crab.

Red Snapper Chinois (page 113)

Tournedos de Saumon
Laurent Quenioux, Seventh Street Bistro

20 cherry tomatoes
1 pound unsalted butter
2 pounds salmon fillets, rolled and tied
3 tablespoons dry white wine
2 shallots, minced
2 tablespoons heavy cream
1 vanilla bean or dash vanilla extract
1 tablespoon olive oil
2 small yellow peppers, diced
1 small green pepper, finely diced
1 small red pepper, finely diced
1 small zucchini, finely diced
2 tablespoons chopped basil
Salt, pepper
2 ounces blue cheese, crumbled
Fresh basil leaves, for garnish

Cut a thin slice from the stem end of the tomatoes, reserving the caps. Hollow out the tomatoes, leaving the shells intact. Sauté shells in 1 tablespoon butter until skins barely soften. Remove from skillet and set aside.

Cut the salmon into 1-inch spirals. Melt ¼ cup butter in the skillet. Add the salmon and sauté for 3 minutes on each side until done. Keep warm.

Place the white wine and shallots in a saucepan. Reduce by three-quarters. Add heavy cream and vanilla bean. Simmer until reduced by half. Discard vanilla bean. Gradually stir in the remaining butter bit by bit until the sauce is smooth. Remove from heat.

Heat the olive oil in a skillet. Sauté the peppers and zucchini with 2 tablespoons chopped basil and salt and pepper to taste until the vegetables are tender, about 30 seconds. Stir in the blue cheese. Spoon into the cherry tomato cavities. Top with caps.

For each serving, spoon some vanilla bean sauce to cover the bottom of each plate. Place 2 slices of sautéed salmon in the center of the plate, and arrange 5 stuffed cherry tomatoes, Olympic-ring fashion, over the salmon. Garnish each plate with fresh basil.

MAKES 4 SERVINGS

Salmon in Raspberry Vinaigrette
Werner Albrecht, Five-Star Catering Co., Inc.

10 ounces fresh salmon
½ cup *Raspberry Vinaigrette* (recipe follows)
1 small red pepper, seeded and minced
½ bunch chives, minced
4 sprigs thyme

Slice the salmon in 20 very thin slices. (Salmon must be fresh, firm, and chilled; otherwise the slices will be too fragile.) Arrange the salmon slices in a fan shape on 4 warm, broiler-proof serving plates, 5 slices per plate. Sprinkle 2 tablespoons raspberry vinaigrette over each serving. Place plates under the broiler for 1½ minutes. Remove from heat and let stand for 1 minute. Place 2 tablespoons minced red pepper and chives at the base of each salmon fan and tuck a sprig of thyme to one side. Serve at once.

MAKES 4 SERVINGS

Raspberry Vinaigrette

3 tablespoons raspberry vinegar
Pinch salt
1½ teaspoons pure crystalline fructose
Pinch freshly ground black pepper
Pinch garlic powder
1 tablespoon Dijon mustard
1 tablespoon fresh lemon juice
½ cup water
2 tablespoons walnut oil

Combine the vinegar, salt, fructose, pepper, garlic powder, mustard, lemon juice, water, and walnut oil in a blender and blend well.

TERRINE OF SALMON, CORN, AND JALAPEÑOS
John Sedlar, St. Estèphe

2 pounds salmon fillets
1⅓ cups heavy cream
2 eggs
Salt, white pepper
2 ears corn, cooked and cut off the cob
4 jalapeño chiles, chopped
1 whole red pepper, roasted and peeled
Green Chile Mayonnaise (recipe follows)

Purée the salmon with the cream in a food processor. Add the eggs and season with salt and pepper. Stir in the corn and chiles.

Fill a 2-quart (9-inch) loaf pan with half the salmon mixture. Cut the red pepper in half and remove seeds. Place red pepper halves down the center of the pâté. Fill with remaining salmon mixture. Cover with a sheet of wax paper and place in another pan filled halfway with hot water. Bake at 350 degrees for 45 minutes. Chill. Unmold and serve sliced with green chile mayonnaise.

MAKES 8 SERVINGS

Green Chile Mayonnaise

4 egg yolks
1 tablespoon cider vinegar
1 teaspoon Dijon mustard
Salt, white pepper
1 cup oil
¼ cup minced jalapeño chiles

Beat together the egg yolks, vinegar, mustard, and salt and pepper until ribbon-thick. Slowly add oil, blending well. Stir in the chiles.

MAKES 2 CUPS

PAUPIETTE DE DOVER SOLE OLYMPIAD
Michel Blanchet, L'Ermitage

1½ pounds Dover sole fillets, cut for 4 portions
Salt, pepper
Salmon Mousse (recipe follows)
4 squares foil, about 8 to 10 inches square
White wine
Fish stock
Saffron Sauce (recipe page 100)
3 or 4 Chinese snow peas

Flatten the sole fillets slightly, using the flat side of a cleaver or wide knife. Sprinkle the skin side with salt and pepper. Spread with a thin coat of salmon mousse. Shape each foil square into a ½-inch-thick tube. Roll each fillet around tube. Add white wine and fish stock to the level of ½ inch in a baking dish large enough to fit all of the rolls. Place the fish rolls in the wine-stock mixture. Bake at 350 degrees for 7 to 8 minutes or until fish fillets are tender, but neither under- nor overcooked.

Remove fillets from liquid and let stand 5 minutes to set before removing foil tube. Remove the tubes, and cut the fillet rolls into ¾-inch-thick rings. Cover the bottom of each of 4 plates with a thin layer of saffron sauce. Arrange the fish rings in the center of the sauce to resemble the rings of the Olympics symbol.

Cut the snow peas into lengthwise strips ¼-inch wide. Arrange them around the rims of the plates to resemble a star.

MAKES 4 SERVINGS

Salmon Mousse

¼ pound salmon fillet
1 cup heavy cream
2 tablespoons butter, softened
2 egg whites
Salt, pepper
Pinch nutmeg

Combine the salmon, cream, soft butter, egg whites, salt and pepper to taste, and nutmeg in a blender. Blend until a smooth paste is formed.

TOP: *Hunan-Style Steamed Fish (page 109)*

BOTTOM, LEFT: *Vegetables for Tournedos de Saumon (page 96)*

BOTTOM, RIGHT: *Paupiette de Dover Sole Olympiad (page 97)*

OPPOSITE: *Grilled Tuna Salad (page 100); Paupiette de Dorade Rouge (page 100)*

Saffron Sauce

2 cups fish stock
¼ cup stewed tomatoes
Pinch ground saffron
1 cup heavy cream
2 tablespoons butter, softened
Salt, pepper

Place the stock in a saucepan. Cook over high heat until the stock is reduced by almost half. Stir in the tomatoes, saffron, and cream. Reduce sauce to ½ of original volume. Place the saffron mixture in a blender. Gradually beat in the butter until smooth. Strain the sauce through a fine sieve. Season to taste with salt and pepper.

PAUPIETTE DE DORADE ROUGE
Susumu Fukui, La Petite Chaya

4 tablespoons oil
4 tablespoons butter or margarine
2 (3-ounce) red snapper fillets
6 to 8 tiny new potatoes, peeled and cut into ovals
3 slices bacon, cut into julienne slices
½ teaspoon minced garlic
1 ounce fresh shiitake mushrooms, cut into 8 wedges
1 ounce fresh chanterelle mushrooms or other forest
   mushrooms, stemmed and quartered
3 cultivated mushrooms, stemmed and quartered
1 teaspoon chopped shallots
¼ cup chablis
Salt, pepper, cayenne pepper
Hosho or parchment paper

Combine 2 tablespoons oil and 2 tablespoons butter in a large skillet. Add the fish fillets and sauté until the fish is lightly browned on both sides, about 5 minutes. Remove from skillet and set aside.

Add 2 tablespoons oil to the skillet. Sauté the potatoes over low heat until golden on all sides. Add enough water to barely cover bottom of pan. Cover and simmer for 5 to 10 minutes, or until potatoes are tender. Remove potatoes and set aside. Add the bacon, garlic, shiitakes, chanterelles, and cultivated mushrooms to the skillet. Sauté until golden and the bacon is crisp.

In a medium saucepan cook the shallots in chablis until soft. Add a few drops of water and 2 tablespoons butter. Cook until a syrupy glaze is formed. Add salt, pepper, and cayenne to taste.

Place each fish fillet on an 8-inch square of hosho or parchment paper. Top with the mushroom-and-bacon mixture, distributing evenly. Spoon some of the sauce over the filling. Fold paper in half to form a half moon. Crimp edges by folding rim over, following contour of curve, to prevent sauce from escaping. Bake at 350 degrees until paper begins to turn golden and puffs up, about 5 to 8 minutes. Make a slit in the paper. Serve at once with the potatoes.

MAKES 2 SERVINGS

GRILLED TUNA SALAD
Ken Frank, La Toque

4 (4-ounce) fresh tuna fillets, cut into 3 x 1½-inch pieces
Green Sauce (recipe follows)
Red Sauce (recipe follows)
4 oba leaves (preserved Japanese red oak)
¼ cup rice vinegar
2 tablespoons mirin
Dash soy sauce
1 teaspoon minced green onion tops
Chili paste
1 cup enoki mushrooms
Sesame seeds or orange roe

Preheat oven broiler or prepare a medium-hot grill. Cook the tuna until browned outside, but still pink inside. (Omit this step if fresh, raw tuna is desired for salad.)

Spoon two tablespoons of green sauce over one-half of each plate. Spoon two tablespoons of red sauce over the other half, being careful to keep from mixing the sauces. Center an oba leaf on each plate over the sauces. Place tuna on the center of each leaf.

Combine rice vinegar, mirin, soy sauce, green onion, and chili paste in a bowl, blending well. Add enoki mushrooms, mixing to coat well. Place about ¼ cup marinated mushrooms over tuna on each plate. Sprinkle with sesame seeds or orange roe.

MAKES 4 SERVINGS

Note: Preserved oba leaves are found in vacuum-sealed packages at Japanese grocery stores. Fresh enoki mushrooms can be found at gourmet food stores and many supermarkets. If fresh tuna is used, shop only at a reputable fish market.

Green Sauce

1 small piece ginger root, peeled and cut up
8-inch hothouse (hydroponic) cucumber, peeled, seeded,
 and cut up
2 green onions, tops only
½ cup rice wine vinegar
½ cup peanut oil
1 teaspoon soy sauce

Combine the ginger, cucumber, and green onion tops in a
blender or food processor. Process 30 seconds. Add rice wine
vinegar, oil, and soy sauce. Blend 20 seconds longer. Use half
the sauce for the red sauce recipe.

Red Sauce

½ recipe *Green Sauce*
1 to 2 teaspoons Chinese plum paste

Blend together the green sauce and plum paste. Process in a
blender or food processor until smooth.

Tuna with Tangerine-Butter Sauce

Joe Venezia, Hotel Bel-Air

2 teaspoons chopped fresh basil
2 teaspoons chopped fennel leaves
2 teaspoons chopped fresh tarragon
2 tablespoons chopped Italian parsley
¼ cup olive oil
2 (6-ounce) pieces fresh tuna
½ cup tangerine juice
¼ cup butter or margarine
Whole basil, fennel, tarragon, and parsley leaves
2 chives with blossoms

Combine the chopped basil, fennel leaves, tarragon, parsley,
and olive oil in a small bowl. Grill the tuna over charcoal until
brown on the outside and pink inside, 1 to 2 minutes,
depending on thickness, basting often with the herb-olive oil
mixture.

Bring the tangerine juice to a boil in a small saucepan.
Whisk in the butter, bit by bit, until the sauce coats the back
of a spoon. Arrange the whole herb leaves in the center of
each plate. Spoon sauce over herbs to cover each plate. Place
tuna over herbs. Garnish with chive stem.

MAKES 2 SERVINGS

Roasted Sea Bass with Crust of Herbs

Bruno Cirino, Antoine, Hotel Meridien, Newport Beach

1 bunch Italian parsley, chopped
1 bunch chervil, chopped
1 sprig thyme, chopped
4 basil leaves, chopped
2½ cups (1¼ pounds) butter, at room temperature
2 cups torn white bread
Salt, pepper
2 pounds sea bass fillets, cut into 6 portions
6 baby Japanese eggplants
6 cherry tomatoes
6 small white onions
6 baby artichokes
6 baby new potatoes
6 baby zucchini flowers
1 medium onion, chopped
2 cloves garlic, minced
1 tablespoon olive oil
½ cup grated Parmesan cheese
2 eggs, lightly beaten
1 bunch chives, chopped

Combine the parsley, chervil, thyme, and basil. Mix the
herbs with 2 cups soft butter, bread, and salt and pepper.
Spread the mixture on each of the 6 fillets. Refrigerate.

Cut off the tops of the eggplants, tomatoes, onions, artichokes, and potatoes; reserve tops. Scoop out the vegetable
cavities using a small teaspoon, and chop the pulp. Set aside.
Rinse the zucchini flowers. Sauté the onion and garlic in oil
until tender. Add the vegetable pulp and sauté 7 minutes or
until tender. Remove from heat and stir in the Parmesan
cheese and eggs, and season with salt and pepper. Mix well.
Cool.

TOP: *Bruno Cirino*

RIGHT: *Roasted Sea Bass with Crust of Herbs (page 101)*

Stuff the vegetable shells with the sautéed vegetable mixture. Place vegetable caps back on shells to cover. Stuff the zucchini flowers with the vegetable mixture, twisting the tips to seal. Tie the vegetables together with string or wood picks, if necessary, to keep filling from falling out during cooking. Place the stuffed vegetables (including the stuffed zucchini flowers) in a skillet large enough to hold them in a single layer. Add water to bottom of pan. Cover, and simmer over medium-low heat for 15 minutes, adding more water if necessary to keep the bottom of the vegetables from scorching. Add 1/2 cup butter to cooking liquid, and stir to blend. Add chives, and season with salt and pepper.

Meanwhile, remove the sea bass fillets from the refrigerator; cook them in a roasting pan at 400 degrees for 8 to 15 minutes, depending on thickness. Then brown under the broiler about 4 inches from heat source for a few minutes, until browned. Place hot sea bass fillets in the center of each plate. Arrange one of each baby vegetable around the fish. Pour the chive sauce over the vegetables.

MAKES 6 SERVINGS

Note: Any seasonal baby vegetables may be used.

SCAMPI MARE NOSTRUM
La Scala

24 large prawns, peeled, deveined, and split lengthwise
Salt, pepper
1/2 cup olive oil
1/2 cup white wine
Juice of 1 lemon
1/2 cup fish or chicken stock
2 large shallots, chopped
2 tablespoons chopped sweet basil
2 tablespoons chopped fresh oregano

Arrange the prawns butterfly-fashion in a baking pan. Season with salt and pepper. Combine the oil, wine, lemon juice, fish or chicken stock, shallots, basil, and oregano. Pour over prawns, turning to coat well. Marinate for 1 hour. When ready to cool, remove the prawns from the marinade, shaking off excess. Place under broiler and broil for 10 minutes or until golden. Do not overcook.

MAKES 6 SERVINGS

SHRIMP WITH GREEN PEPPERCORN SAUCE
Joe Allen

24 large shrimp
1 1/2 tablespoons olive oil
1 1/2 tablespoons butter
1/4 cup brandy
1 shallot, minced
1/4 teaspoon minced garlic
2 1/2 tablespoons green peppercorns
1 cup heavy cream
1/4 cup sour cream
Salt, white pepper
1 bunch dill, chopped

Peel the shrimp, leaving tails intact. Heat the oil and butter in a large pan. Add the shrimp and sauté for 4 to 5 minutes or until shrimp turn pink. Remove shrimp and keep warm.

Deglaze the pan with brandy, then add the shallot, garlic, and green peppercorns. Reduce liquid by half or until slightly thickened. Add the cream. Boil until reduced by half. Remove from heat. Whisk in the sour cream. Season to taste with salt and white pepper.

Return shrimp to pan and toss to coat well with sauce, and reheat. Fold in the dill.

MAKES 6 SERVINGS

SAUTÉ OF SQUID, SHRIMP, AND EGGPLANT
Bob Brody, Sheraton Harbor Island West, San Diego

2 medium eggplants
Salt
1 small squid, cleaned
16 large shrimp
1 red pepper
1 green pepper
4 tomatoes
Olive oil
3 cloves garlic, minced
1 teaspoon chile powder
Juice of 1 lemon

Peel the eggplants and slice into ¼-inch-thick slices lengthwise. Sprinkle with salt on both sides and chill for 1 hour to allow bitter flavors to leach out. Cut into ¼-inch strips, reserving 4 whole slices.

Cut the body of the squid into ½-inch diagonal slices; keep the tentacle section whole. Reserve.

Shell and devein the shrimp. Cut the red and green peppers into ⅛-inch strips. Peel and seed the tomato and chop coarsely.

Heat 2 tablespoons olive oil in skillet until hot. Add the reserved 4 whole slices eggplant and cook until golden brown on both sides. Do not overcook. Remove from heat and keep warm. Reduce heat and add pepper strips and garlic, adding more oil as needed. Sauté for 1 minute. Add the squid, reserved tentacles, shrimp, and eggplant strips. Cook until the shrimp turn pink. Add the chile powder and tomatoes. Continue to simmer gently. Add salt and lemon juice to taste.

Remove from heat. Place a slice of eggplant on each plate. Spoon the shrimp mixture over the eggplant.

MAKES 4 SERVINGS

SCALLOPS WITH LIME BUTTER
The First Street Bar and Grill, Claremont

2 pounds scallops
Flour
2 tablespoons almond oil
1 cup dry white wine
1 cup heavy cream
¼ cup unsalted butter, softened
Juice of 3 limes
Salt, pepper
Lime slices, for garnish

Dust the scallops lightly with flour, and shake off any excess. Heat the oil in a large skillet. Add the scallops and brown lightly — the center should be slightly translucent. Remove the scallops from the pan and keep warm.

Pour off excess oil from the skillet and add the white wine. Reduce the wine until the pan is glazed and syrupy. Stir in the cream and reduce until cream has thickened slightly. Turn heat to low and whisk in the softened butter and lime juice. Season to taste with salt and pepper. Pour over scallops and garnish with lime slices.

MAKES 8 SERVINGS

STUFFED SCALLOP SURPRISE WITH SAFFRON SAUCE
Patrick Healy, Colette, Beverly Pavilion Hotel

4 to 6 jumbo sea scallops, about 1 pound
2 bunches spinach, large leaves only
1 carrot
1 turnip
1 yellow squash
1 zucchini
2 tablespoons unsalted butter
Salt, pepper
Saffron Sauce (recipe page 106)
1 ripe tomato, blanched, seeded, and finely cubed
1 bunch chives, chopped

Clean the scallops and remove the muscles. Slice scallops horizontally to make three equal slices for each scallop. Clean and stem the spinach. Blanch the leaves for 30 seconds in boiling salted water. Plunge into iced water. Peel the carrot and the turnip, and cut into medium julienne strips. Using only the skin of the yellow squash and zucchini, cut it into medium julienne strips.

Melt 1 tablespoon butter over low heat and add the julienned vegetables. Cover and steam for 1 minute. Drain in a strainer, and set aside. Lightly season the scallop slices with salt and pepper. Spoon about 1 teaspoon julienned vegetable mixture on each of the scallop slices. Top with remaining scallop slices to make a two-decker sandwich, or top with another teaspoon julienned vegetables and close with remaining scallop slice for a three-decker sandwich. Wrap each scallop sandwich in one or two blanched spinach leaves, keeping shiny side exposed. Melt the remaining butter in a skillet large enough to hold the scallop bundles. Add the scallops, cover, and steam-cook for 3 to 4 minutes.

Spoon the saffron sauce on a platter to cover the bottom. Arrange the scallop bundles down the center of the sauce. Sprinkle with finely chopped tomato cubes and chives. Garnish with any remaining vegetables, if desired.

MAKES 4 TO 6 SERVINGS

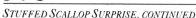

Saffron Sauce

3 tablespoons unsalted butter
1 shallot, minced
2 cups white wine
1 teaspoon saffron threads
1½ cups heavy cream
Salt, pepper

Melt 2 tablespoons butter in a saucepan. Add the shallot and cook until barely tender. Add the wine and saffron and reduce liquid by one-third. Stir in the cream and cook over low heat for 6 to 7 minutes, stirring constantly. Whisk in remaining butter just before serving. Add salt and pepper to taste.

Lobster with Wild Watercress Dressing
Joe Venezia, Hotel Bel-Air

½ cup *each*: fresh laurel (bay leaf), chervil, sorrel, tarragon, basil, fennel, Italian parsley (see note)
1 cup white vermouth
1 (2- to 3-pound) lobster
Wild Watercress Dressing (recipe follows)
1 tomato, cut julienne
1 small sweet yellow pepper, cut julienne
1 small sweet red pepper, cut julienne
Additional fresh herbs, for garnish

Scatter the herbs in the bottom of a large saucepan. Add white vermouth. Top with the lobster. Cover and bring to a boil. Steam until lobster is done, about 20 to 25 minutes.

Remove lobster from pan. Crack shells and claws (if any). Pour some of the watercress sauce on the bottom of the platter. Arrange the lobster tail and claws over the sauce. Combine the tomato and the sweet yellow and red peppers, and toss with the remaining wild watercress dressing. Place around the lobster. Garnish with additional herbs.

MAKES 2 SERVINGS

Note: If any of the fresh herbs listed above are not available, choose any seasonal herbs desired.

Wild Watercress Dressing

1 sprig chervil
1 bunch wild watercress (Upland watercress), stems trimmed
½ small Spanish onion, chopped
¼ cup chardonnay wine vinegar
1 egg yolk
¼ cup olive oil
Salt, freshly ground white pepper

In a food processor or blender combine the chervil, watercress, onion, wine vinegar, egg yolk, olive oil, and salt and pepper to taste. Blend until the mixture is emulsified, being careful not to blend too much or dressing will separate.

MAKES ABOUT ½ CUP

Stir-Fried Oysters with Garlic and Green Onions
Mon Kee Restaurant

1 pound oysters, shucked
1 teaspoon cornstarch
1 teaspoon oyster sauce
1½ teaspoons soy sauce
⅛ teaspoon salt
1 tablespoon oil
½ teaspoon white wine
2 cloves garlic, minced
2 green onions, cut into 2-inch pieces
1 slice ginger root, chopped

Bring 4 cups of water in a large saucepan to a boil. Plunge the oysters into the boiling water. Cook 10 to 15 seconds, until edges begin to curl. Remove with a slotted spoon to paper towels to drain.

Blend together the cornstarch and 2 tablespoons water until smooth. Stir in the oyster sauce, soy sauce, and salt. Set aside.

Heat the oil in a wok until hot. Add the wine, oysters, garlic, green onions, and ginger. Stir-fry 15 seconds. Drain off any excess liquid that accumulates. Stir in reserved sauce. Stir-fry 1 minute, just until sauce bubbles and thickens.

MAKES 4 SERVINGS

*Joe Venezia with his Lobster with Wild Watercress Dressing
(recipe this page)*

Corn Mousse with Clams

(*Mousse de Maïs aux Palourdes*)
Joachim Splichal, Max au Triangle

2 ears corn
1 pound littleneck clams (about 8)
2 tablespoons white wine
1 shallot, peeled and halved
1 tablespoon chopped parsley
3 eggs, beaten
3/4 cup heavy cream
Salt, pepper
Nutmeg
Chanterelle Sauce (recipe follows)

Cut the corn kernels off the cob and blanch in boiling water for 1 minute. Drain and set aside. Steam the clams, covered, with the white wine and shallot just until clams open, about 5 minutes. Shell the clams and chop. Reserve liquid for the chanterelle sauce.

Divide the corn kernels, chopped clams, and parsley among 4 buttered shallow baking dishes, about 4 inches in diameter. Beat the eggs and cream in a bowl until blended. Season to taste with salt, pepper, and nutmeg. Pour over the clam mixture. Bake at 350 degrees for 25 to 35 minutes or until done. Serve with the chanterelle sauce.

MAKES 4 SERVINGS

Chanterelle Sauce

Reserved clam liquid
1/2 cup plus 1 tablespoon unsalted butter
3/4 cup julienne-cut chanterelle mushrooms (see note)
1/4 cup finely chopped chives

Heat the clam liquid over low heat. Slowly add 1/2 cup butter, cut into cubes. Beat with a whisk or place in a blender or processor and combine until smooth. Heat remaining 1 tablespoon butter in a skillet. Add the mushrooms and sauté 5 minutes. Add the clam sauce and chives, and stir to combine.

MAKES ABOUT 1 1/2 CUPS

Note: Fresh chanterelles are available at gourmet groceries. If using dried mushrooms, reconstitute in warm water 10 minutes before using.

Poached Chilled Salmon

1 onion, sliced
2 stalks celery
1 cup water
1/4 teaspoon salt
3 pounds fresh salmon
Watercress sprigs, for garnish
Watercress Sauce (recipe follows)

Combine the onion, celery, water, and salt in a large poaching pan or shallow pan. Add the salmon. Bring to a boil, reduce heat, and cover. Cook for 30 to 35 minutes, or until salmon is opaque and flakes with a fork.

Cool salmon in the poaching liquid. Carefully transfer to a large platter. Garnish with watercress sprigs and serve with the watercress sauce.

MAKES 6 TO 8 SERVINGS

Watercress Sauce

1/2 cup sour cream
1/2 cup mayonnaise
1 bunch chopped watercress leaves (do not use the stems)
1 teaspoon lemon juice
Salt, pepper

Combine the sour cream, mayonnaise, watercress, lemon juice, and salt and pepper to taste. Chill until ready to serve.

MAKES ABOUT 1 CUP

Grilled Salmon Fillets in Lettuce

4 (4- to 6-ounce) salmon fillets
3 tablespoons lemon juice
2 tablespoons white wine
4 teaspoons olive oil
3 tablespoons capers
1/4 teaspoon dry mustard
Salt
16 leaves green leaf lettuce
Mustard Sauce (recipe follows)

Rinse the salmon with cold water. Pat dry with paper towels, and set aside. Combine the lemon juice, white wine, olive oil, capers, and mustard. Season to taste with salt. Pour over the salmon and marinate 30 minutes, turning once. Reserve marinade.

Blanch the lettuce leaves in boiling water for 5 seconds. Drain well. Arrange 2 leaves with the stem ends overlapping at the center. Spoon about 2 teaspoons of the marinade over the lettuce. Place 1 salmon fillet on the lettuce. Top with 1 or 2 more teaspoons marinade, including some of capers. Roll fillet up. Place 2 leaves on top and tuck edges under fish. Bring up the bottom leaf edges. Tie package-style with string. Repeat with remaining lettuce, marinade, and fillets to make 4 packages in all.

Place the salmon bundles on a well-greased grill 4 to 5 inches from hot coals, and cook 5 to 6 minutes. Turn and cook an additional 5 to 6 minutes. Remove string and serve with mustard sauce, if desired.

MAKES 4 SERVINGS

Mustard Sauce

2 tablespoons butter or margarine
1 1/2 teaspoons flour
1/4 cup vinegar
1/4 cup boiling water
1/2 bouillon cube
1/4 cup dry mustard
1 tablespoon sugar
1 egg, beaten

Blend the butter and flour in the top of a double boiler until smooth. Add the vinegar, boiling water, bouillon cube half, mustard, sugar, and egg. Cook and stir over hot water until sauce thickens, about 10 minutes.

BAKED CATFISH FILLETS WITH HORSERADISH SAUCE

1 to 1 1/2 pounds catfish fillets, cut into 4 portions
1 tablespoon lemon juice
2 egg whites
2 tablespoons sour cream
1 tablespoon grated onion
1 clove garlic

1/4 teaspoon dry mustard
1/4 teaspoon white pepper
2 tablespoons butter or margarine
2 tablespoons flour
1 cup milk
4 teaspoons prepared horseradish

Arrange the fish on a baking pan sprayed with nonstick cooking spray. Sprinkle with lemon juice. In a small bowl beat the egg whites until soft peaks form. Fold in the sour cream, onion, garlic, mustard, and 1/8 teaspoon white pepper. Spoon some of the mixture on top of each fillet. Bake at 375 degrees for 20 minutes or until fish is opaque or a skewer glides easily through flesh.

Meanwhile in a small saucepan melt the butter, then blend in the flour until smooth. Stir in the milk, horseradish, and remaining 1/8 teaspoon white pepper. Cook and stir over medium heat until mixture is bubbly and slightly thickened. Serve over the fish.

MAKES 4 SERVINGS

HUNAN-STYLE STEAMED FISH
(To Sze Tsen Yui)

1 1/2- to 2-pound freshwater fish, such as carp
2 ounces Chinese fermented black beans
2 small, fresh, hot, red chiles, finely chopped
1/2 teaspoon minced ginger root
1/2 teaspoon minced garlic
2 green onions, chopped
Salt, optional
1 to 2 teaspoons sherry
1 tablespoon lard or 2 tablespoons oil

Wash the fish and pat dry. Cut one long diagonal slit or several crosswise slits in each side. Sprinkle the fish inside and out with salt to taste. Place the fish on a platter for steaming.

Rinse the black beans and drain, and chop coarsely if desired. Combine the black beans, chiles, ginger, garlic, and onions. Spread the bean mixture on top of the fish, and sprinkle with the sherry. Set the lard on the fish or sprinkle with oil. Place the fish in a steamer and steam, covered, 15 to 20 minutes or until fish flakes easily.

MAKES 4 TO 6 SERVINGS

TOP: *Tuna with Tangerine-Butter Sauce (page 101)*
BOTTOM: *Stuffed Scallop Surprise with Saffron Sauce (page 105)*
RIGHT: *Fillet Mosaic with Red Pepper Sauce (page 112)*

FILLET MOSAIC WITH RED PEPPER SAUCE

1½ pounds thin sole fillets
½ pound thin salmon fillets
12 large spinach leaves, washed
2 cups fish or chicken stock
1 shallot, minced
½ cup dry white wine
2 large red peppers, roasted, peeled, and puréed
1 tablespoon apple jelly
1 tablespoon lemon juice
Salt, pepper

Cut the sole into twenty-four ½-inch-wide strips, about 5 inches long. Cut the salmon fillets into twelve ½-inch-wide strips 5 inches long. Trim the stems from the spinach leaves. Blanch the spinach in hot water for about 3 seconds to soften. Drain. Roll lengthwise as thinly as possible.

To prepare each serving, place 6 sole strips lengthwise side by side. Tightly weave a spinach strip among the sole strips at the top. Below that weave a salmon strip. Now weave in another spinach strip. Continue to alternately weave the salmon and spinach strips. You will need 3 salmon strips and 3 spinach strips for each sole mosaic. Continue to weave remaining 3 portions. Set aside.

Place the stock and shallots in a skillet large enough to hold the fish squares. Bring to a boil, then reduce heat. Using a wide slotted spatula, place the fish squares into the hot broth. Cover and simmer over very low heat 5 minutes. Carefully remove. Keep warm. If your skillet is not large enough to hold all of the fish, cook them in batches.

Skim any white residue from the remaining broth in the skillet. Add the wine to the broth, and simmer over high heat until the broth is reduced by half. Stir in the red pepper purée, the apple jelly, and lemon juice, and season to taste with salt and pepper. Strain the sauce, then nap the bottom of a serving platter or individual plates with some, and cover with the sole squares.

MAKES 4 SERVINGS

CALIFORNIA BOUILLABAISSE

½ cup oil
2 cloves garlic, minced
1 large onion, sliced
1 or 2 leeks, thinly sliced
1 bay leaf
2 cups peeled and chopped tomatoes
2 cups fish stock or 1 cup water and 1 cup clam juice
1 cup dry white wine
¼ cup chopped fresh fennel or ½ teaspoon crushed fennel seeds
⅛ teaspoon crushed saffron threads
1 teaspoon salt
¼ teaspoon black pepper
2 tablespoons minced parsley
2 lobster tails, split through the shells
1 pound red snapper, cut in chunks
1 pound halibut or sea bass, cut in chunks
12 medium shrimp
6 Dungeness crab legs
6 clams
6 oysters
6 mussels

Heat the oil in a large pot. Add the garlic, onion, leeks, and bay leaf, and cook until the onion is tender but not browned. Add the tomatoes, stock, wine, fennel, saffron, salt, pepper, and parsley. Bring to a boil. Reduce heat and simmer about 5 minutes. Then add the lobster, snapper, and halibut, and cook for 10 minutes.

Meanwhile, rinse the shrimp and crab, and scrub the clams, oysters, and mussels. Add the shellfish to the pot and cook 5 minutes or until shells open. Ladle into large soup plates and serve with crusty bread.

MAKES 6 TO 8 SERVINGS

CRACKED CRAB NORTH BEACH

5 to 6 large crabs, preferably fresh
1 tablespoon salt
1 onion, quartered
1 bay leaf
Vinegar
Vinaigrette, lemon, or mayonnaise

Plunge live crabs into 5 to 6 quarts boiling water seasoned with the salt, onion, bay leaf, and 1 tablespoon vinegar per quart water. Bring again to a boil. Cover and cook for 8 to 10 minutes. Drain and plunge crabs into cold water, drain again, and cool.

Twist off claws and legs close to bodies. Pry off the back of each shell by inserting a table knife. Remove spongy parts, then rinse body meat under running water. Cut into four pieces with poultry shears or a heavy knife. Discard top shell. Crack the claws and legs by rapping sharply with a kitchen mallet. Chill crab thoroughly.

Arrange the claws, legs, and body pieces on cracked ice. (If using frozen crab meat, thaw before arranging on ice.) Place a small cup vinaigrette, lemon, or mayonnaise in the center or off to the side. Use as dip for crab. Have nut or lobster crackers and seafood forks available.

MAKES 5 TO 6 SERVINGS

RED SNAPPER CHINOIS

1 to 1 1/2 pounds red snapper or other firm-fleshed fish
Salt, pepper
1/4 cup flour
2 tablespoons peanut oil
1 small onion, chopped
3 tablespoons dry white wine or mirin
1/2 pound Chinese snow peas
1/2 cup chopped cilantro leaves
Lime wedges, for garnish

Season the fish fillets with salt and pepper to taste. Dredge the fish in flour. Heat the oil in a skillet, add the onion and sauté until tender. Add the fish fillets and lightly brown on both sides, allowing about 2 minutes on each side. Add the wine and snow peas. Cover and simmer over medium heat for 5 minutes until the snow peas turn bright green. Remove fish and snow peas to a warm platter. Add the cilantro leaves to the skillet. Stir-fry for 1 minute until wilted. Spoon over fish fillets. Serve with wedges of lime, if desired.

MAKES 4 TO 6 SERVINGS

OVERLEAF: *California Bouillabaisse (page 112)*

POULTRY AND GAME

PLUMPED POUSSIN
Laura Chenel and Linda Siegfried

CHICKEN PAILLARD WITH ANCHO CHILI BUTTER
Jeremiah Tower, Stars, San Francisco

FUN SEE CHICKEN
Madame Wu's Garden

CHICKEN BURGER
Bistro Garden

PAN-ROASTED QUAILS WITH HARD CIDER
Cindy Black, Piret's, San Diego

QUAILS WITH SUMMER VEGETABLES
Michael's

SMOKE-ROASTED SQUAB WITH RED WINE SAUCE
Jeremiah Tower, Stars, San Francisco

MINCED SQUAB
(Chinese Tacos)
The Mandarin

PIGEON WITH CHANTERELLES AND BABY
  CALIFORNIA VEGETABLES
L'Orangerie

TRUMPS CUBAN SANDWICH
Michael Roberts, Trumps

GRILLED GAME HENS

ORANGE HONEYED CHICKEN

STIR-FRIED CHICKEN AND ZUCCHINI

DUCKLING WITH MOLE SAUCE

ARROZ CON POLLO Á LA CUBANA

Nowhere in America has the focus on health been sharper than in California. When the word went out that red meats had a slightly higher fat content than chicken, health-conscious diners and cooks here sharply reduced their intake of steak in favor of more poultry. There is an increasing taste for delicate meats, and you will find in this chapter imaginative recipes featuring not only chicken but quail, squabs, game hens, and ducklings, many of them reflecting the exotic food styles that have set their stamp on California cuisine.

In Chinatown one can buy a freshly slaughtered chicken or take one home fully cooked. Outside of Los Angeles, specially grown full-breasted ducks are raised, as well as mallards whose over-sized, silky smooth livers have become another sought-after product by the region's chefs, and are now finding their way into home kitchens.

But a master chef does not need ingredients as elegant as breast of duck or foie gras in order to create a memorable dish. Laura Chenel and Linda Siegfried serve a chicken with the local Sonoma Valley goat cheese stuffed between the skin and flesh (Plumped Poussin, page 117), that is one of the stylistic marks of the new California cuisine.

PLUMPED POUSSIN
Laura Chenel and Linda Siegfried

2 small young chickens or 2 game hens
2 cloves garlic, minced
2 teaspoons lemon juice
Olive oil
1 teaspoon chopped fresh thyme, rosemary, or parsley
¼ teaspoon salt
¼ teaspoon black pepper
1 ounce chèvre, approximately

For each bird, carefully slip fingers between the skin and breast meat on each side of the breastbone to loosen the skin. Combine the garlic, lemon juice, 2 tablespoons olive oil, thyme, salt, and pepper. Sprinkle the chicken cavities with some of the garlic mixture, then insert the rest in small pockets under the skin on each side of the breastbone of the birds. Add goat cheese under the skin as well. Rub the birds with olive oil or butter and place on a rack in a baking pan. Bake at 375 degrees for 1 hour, basting with pan juices every 15 minutes.

MAKES 2 SERVINGS

CHICKEN PAILLARD WITH ANCHO CHILI BUTTER
Jeremiah Tower, Stars, San Francisco

3 whole chicken breasts, split, boned, and skinned
¼ cup olive oil
2 to 3 tablespoons ancho chili powder
¾ cup unsalted butter, softened
Salt
Grilled Vegetables (recipe follows)
12 lemon or lime wedges, for garnish

Place the chicken breasts between 2 pieces of wax paper and pound with the side of a cleaver until thin. Combine the olive oil with 1 tablespoon of the chili powder in a dish just large enough to hold the chicken in one layer. Add chicken to oil mixture, turning once to coat well. Cover and marinate, refrigerated, 3 hours.

In a small bowl, combine softened butter with 1 to 2 tablespoons chili powder. Season to taste with salt. Set aside. Butter should be soft when served.

At serving time, remove chicken from marinade and cook over medium coals about 1 minute per side. Remove to warm plates, top the chicken with a dollop of ancho chili butter, and surround with grilled vegetables. Garnish with lemon wedges.

MAKES 6 SERVINGS

Grilled Vegetables

Fennel, red peppers, summer squash, eggplant, mushrooms, and any other vegetables desired

Clean and trim the fennel. Halve the peppers and remove the seeds and inner membranes. Trim the ends from the squash and halve if large. Trim the ends from the eggplants and cut them in thick slices or chunks. Clean the mushrooms. Parboil all the vegetables until barely tender, then drain well.

Place on a grill over medium coals. When the vegetables are done, remove them to a platter and keep warm while chicken is cooking.

Note: Large vegetables, such as fennel and eggplant, will take longer to grill, so start them first and add the rest according to length of time it will take them to cook.

FUN SEE CHICKEN
Madame Wu's Garden

4 ounces *fun see* (bean threads or vermicelli)
3 tablespoons plus ½ teaspoon vegetable oil
½ teaspoon cornstarch
1 tablespoon dark Chinese soy sauce
1 teaspoon light Chinese soy sauce
1 cup thinly sliced dark chicken meat
1 clove garlic, crushed
½ cup Chinese black mushrooms
1 cup thinly sliced Chinese cabbage
½ cup thinly sliced bamboo shoots
2 cups bean sprouts
½ cup snow peas
¼ teaspoon sugar, optional

Plumped Poussin (page 117)

Soak the *fun see* in cold water for 20 minutes. Drain and set aside. There should be 2 cups noodles. Combine ½ teaspoon oil, cornstarch, and both soy sauces; add the chicken, and let stand 20 minutes.

Heat a wok or skillet and add 3 tablespoons oil, coating bottom of pan. Rub the surface of the pan with the garlic clove, then discard. Add the marinated chicken and its marinade, and stir-fry over high heat for 3 minutes. Add the mushrooms and stir 1 minute. Add the cabbage and stir-fry 2 minutes, then the bamboo shoots and bean sprouts, stir-frying them 1 minute. Add 2 cups water, cover, and bring to a boil. Remove cover, add the *fun see*, and stir well to combine. Cover for 1 minute. Remove cover, add the snow peas, and stir-fry for 1 minute. Quickly stir in the sugar, if using, and remove from heat. Serve at once.

MAKES 4 TO 6 SERVINGS

CHICKEN BURGER
Bistro Garden

4 boned and skinned chicken breast halves or 1 (2½-pound)
  chicken, boned and skinned
1 pound lean veal
1 tablespoon chopped parsley
1½ teaspoons salt
½ teaspoon white pepper
Dash Worcestershire sauce
Few drops hot pepper sauce
2 slices white bread
¼ cup hot milk
1 egg
2 tablespoons oil
1 medium onion, sliced
¼ pound mushrooms, sliced
1 bay leaf
Pinch fresh thyme
1 cup dried bread crumbs
¼ cup butter
Mustard Sauce (recipe follows)

Grind together the chicken and veal. Stir in the parsley, salt, white pepper, Worcestershire, and hot pepper sauce. Soak the bread in the milk and add to the meat mixture along with the egg, mixing well.

Heat the oil, add the onion, and cook until barely tender. Add the mushrooms, bay leaf, and thyme. Sauté until the liquid has evaporated. Remove bay leaf. Add the mushroom sauté to the meat mixture. Combine, stirring 2 to 4 minutes; or combine in a food processor until almost smooth. Form into patties and dip in bread crumbs. Melt the butter in a large skillet and add the patties. Cook until browned on both sides, then remove from skillet. When ready to serve, place browned patties in a baking pan and bake at 375 degrees for 10 minutes to crisp. Serve with mustard sauce.

MAKES 6 TO 8 SERVINGS

Mustard Sauce

3 tablespoons Dijon mustard
1 tablespoon Coleman's mustard
1 tablespoon oil
½ onion, chopped
½ stalk celery, chopped
¼ cup white wine vinegar
2 cups brown stock
Pinch salt
½ tablespoon crushed black pepper
Dash Worcestershire sauce

Mix together the mustards. Heat the oil and in it sauté the onion and celery until tender. Add the vinegar and reduce by half. Stir in the mustard mixture and brown stock. Cook 30 minutes. Add salt, pepper, and Worcestershire sauce. Strain into a sauceboat.

MAKES ABOUT 1½ CUPS

PAN-ROASTED QUAILS WITH HARD CIDER
Cindy Black, Piret's, San Diego

12 (3-ounce) whole quails
Salt and pepper to taste
6 tablespoons clarified butter (see note)
1 cup hard cider
Baked Turnips and Cream (recipe follows)

Season the quails with salt and pepper. Sauté them in butter until golden brown. Remove excess fat from pan. Cover and cook over low heat until the quails are tender. Remove quails from pan and keep warm. Add hard cider to pan juices, scraping brown bits from bottom and sides of pan. Cook vigorously until liquid is reduced by one-quarter. Serve the quails with pan juices and baked turnips and cream.

MAKES 6 SERVINGS

Note: For instructions on clarifying butter, see page 33.

Baked Turnips and Cream

1/2 cup cubed bacon
6 medium turnips, peeled and sliced 1/8-inch thick
3 leeks, white portion only, cleaned and sliced
3 cups heavy cream
3 tablespoons Dijon mustard
2 teaspoons ground nutmeg
Salt and pepper to taste

Cook bacon until almost crisp. Drain. Layer raw turnips with bacon and leeks in a baking pan. Combine the cream, mustard, nutmeg, and salt and pepper in a small bowl. Pour over turnips and leeks. Bake at 350 degrees for 1 1/4 to 1 1/2 hours, or until turnips are tender.

MAKES 6 SERVINGS

QUAILS WITH SUMMER VEGETABLES
Michael's

4 fresh quails
2 tablespoons butter, melted
Salt, pepper
4 tablespoons goose liver pâté
8 baby zucchini
8 baby eggplants
3 bunches arugula
12 baby patty pan squash
Potato Pancakes (recipe follows)
Madeira Sauce (recipe follows)

Clean the quails. Brush with the melted butter and sprinkle with salt and pepper to taste. Stuff each quail with 1 tablespoon goose liver pâté. Place in a baking pan and bake at 400 degrees for 20 minutes or until quails are tender.

While the quails are baking, blanch the zucchini, eggplants, arugula, and patty pan squash separately by adding to boiling salted water and simmering about 1 to 4 minutes, depending on the vegetable. Drain and plunge in ice water to keep the vegetables from cooking further. Place the potato pancakes in the center of a large platter or individually on 4 plates. Top with the quails, and around them arrange the blanched vegetables. Spoon the madeira sauce over the quails just before serving.

MAKES 4 SERVINGS

Potato Pancakes

2 large new potatoes
1 egg
2 strips bacon, diced
1/2 cup butter

Peel and cut the potatoes into fine, julienne strips. Place the strips in bowl and add the egg and bacon. Mix well. Divide the potato mixture into 4 portions, and press each into a pancake. Heat 2 tablespoons butter in each of 4 individual (3- or 4-inch) round-bottomed pans. Add the potatoes to the pans and sauté until browned on both sides.

MAKES 4 PANCAKES

Note: If you don't have 4 pancake pans, use 1 small crêpe pan and cook 1 pancake at a time, keeping cooked pancakes warm.

Madeira Sauce

1 cup madeira
1 tablespoon truffle juice, optional
2 tablespoons meat glaze (concentrated veal or beef stock)
1 tablespoon diced goose liver
2 tablespoons butter

Combine the madeira and truffle juice in a saucepan. Heat until reduced by two-thirds. Stir in the meat glaze and cook, stirring, until well blended. Add the goose liver and stir in the butter just until it has melted.

MAKES ABOUT 1/2 CUP

Note: Truffle juice from canned truffles is available at gourmet food stores.

SMOKE-ROASTED SQUAB WITH RED WINE SAUCE

Jeremiah Tower, Stars, San Francisco

4 squabs
Fresh thyme
6 tablespoons olive oil
Salt, pepper
1 cup cabernet or zinfandel wine
8 cups veal, veal-chicken, or duck stock
2 tablespoons unsalted butter

Clean the squabs and truss. In a large pan, combine the thyme and ¼ cup olive oil. Season to taste with salt and pepper. Add squabs to the mixture, turning to coat well. Let stand in a cool, dry spot for 2 hours.

Meanwhile, prepare a covered grill by letting coals burn down to gray ash. Spread coals around the edges and place a drip pan in the center at fuel level to catch drippings from the squabs. Add grapevine cuttings or fruitwood chips to the charcoal and reduce the heat to low. (Heat can be controlled by opening and closing vents in a covered smoker.)

Brown the marinated birds well in remaining 2 tablespoons olive oil in a heavy 3-quart sauté pan. Season to taste with additional thyme. Place the browned birds on the grill over the drip pan in the smoker, reserving browned bits and any oil remaining in the pan. Cover grill, and smoke over low heat for about 1 hour (less for rare squab). Remove birds from smoker and set aside to cool.

When cool, halve and bone the squabs. Chop carcasses and add to the sauté pan. Degrease the pan drippings from the smoker; then add to the sauté pan with the wine and stock. Simmer over medium heat for 30 minutes. Strain and degrease sauce. Return sauce to sauté pan.

When ready to serve, place the boned squabs in the warm (not hot) sauce and let heat through slowly. (Sauce must not boil or the birds will become tough.) When squabs are hot, remove to a serving platter, whisk the butter into the sauce and spoon some of it over the squabs. Any remaining sauce may be served on the side.

MAKES 4 SERVINGS

Note: Wood cuttings or chips may be soaked in water for about 30 minutes before use, if desired.

Jeremiah Tower

Minced Squab

(*Chinese Tacos*)
The Mandarin

Oil for frying
1/4 (8-ounce) package rice noodles
1 tablespoon soy sauce
1 tablespoon Worcestershire sauce
1 1/2 teaspoons sesame oil
Pinch sugar
Pinch white pepper
4 squab, boned (reserve bones and skin for soup or stock)
4 ounces dried black mushrooms
1 (3- or 4-ounce) can water chestnuts
3 or 4 green onions
1 ounce Virginia or other baked ham
1 tomato, cut in wedges (see note)
1 head iceberg lettuce
Cilantro sprigs
Oyster Sauce, optional (recipe follows)

Add enough oil to a depth of 1 inch in a wok or large skillet and heat until hot. Add noodles and fry until puffed, but not golden, about 1 to 3 seconds. Remove at once from the wok, drain on paper towels, and set aside.

Combine the soy sauce, Worcestershire sauce, sesame oil, sugar, and pepper in a small bowl. Set aside.

Mince the squab flesh. Soften the mushrooms in warm water for 5 minutes, then drain. Mince the mushrooms, water chestnuts, green onions, and ham.

Heat 1/2 cup oil in a wok or skillet. Add the minced squab and ham and sauté 1 minute. Add half the soy sauce mixture and sauté until squab is done, about 1 minute. Remove from wok and set aside.

Add the mushrooms and water chestnuts. Sauté 30 seconds, then add the remaining sauce mixture and sauté 30 seconds longer. Remove from wok and add to minced squab mixture. Next sauté the green onions for 30 seconds. Add to minced squab mixture.

Cut off 1/4 of the lettuce head at the stem end. Plunge larger portion in cold water to help the leaves open. Remove the individual leaves, reserving the curled inner portion for other uses.

Crush the fried noodles and place on a serving platter. Make a well in the center, and in it place the squab mixture. Garnish with tomato wedges or "tomato butterflies" and cilantro sprigs. Arrange the lettuce cups on a separate platter.

To serve, spoon a heaping tablespoon or two of the squab mixture in the center of each lettuce cup. Fold it in half like a taco using the oyster sauce for drizzling or dipping, if desired.

MAKES 4 TO 6 SERVINGS

Note: To form a butterfly shape with a tomato, cut a tomato wedge lengthwise in the center, cutting almost but not quite completely in half. Cut peel almost to stem. Do not remove.

Oyster Sauce

1 tablespoon soy sauce
2 tablespoons canned oyster sauce
Pinch white pepper
Pinch sugar

Combine the soy sauce, oyster sauce, pepper, and sugar.

Pigeon with Chanterelles and Baby California Vegetables
L'Orangerie

5 ounces chanterelles
4 baby carrots
4 baby turnips
4 baby zucchini
2 (14- to 17-ounce) pigeons
Salt, pepper
3 tablespoons butter
2 cloves garlic, minced
4 or 5 thyme sprigs, leaves removed
1 cup heavy cream
2 quail eggs, peeled, for garnish

Cook chanterelles in a small amount of water until tender, about 1 to 2 minutes depending on size and thickness. Remove and set aside. Parboil the carrots, turnips, and zucchini in boiling salted water to cover, 1 to 4 minutes. Drain and set aside.

Cut each pigeon into quarters. Season with salt and pepper. Melt 1 tablespoon butter in a skillet. Add pigeon sections and sauté until browned on all sides, about 2 to 3 minutes each side. Set aside.

Melt 1½ teaspoons butter in a saucepan. Add garlic and thyme. Sauté 1 minute. Add cream. Cook until reduced by one-third. Stir in 1½ teaspoons butter, and salt to taste. Keep warm.

In another saucepan, melt remaining 1 tablespoon butter. Lightly sauté the chanterelles, carrots, turnips, and zucchini.

Slice pigeon breasts. Place chanterelles in center of platter. Top with overlapping pigeon breast slices. Surround with the carrots, turnips, and zucchini. Spoon cream sauce over pigeon. Slice or halve the quail eggs, and use to garnish the plate.

MAKES 2 SERVINGS

TRUMPS CUBAN SANDWICH
Michael Roberts, Trumps

Butter or margarine
1 large white onion, thinly sliced
1 large loaf French bread (Parisienne)
Mustard
Mayonnaise
2 cups *Poultry* or *Meat Salad Filling*, or *Seafood Salad Filling* (recipes follow)

Melt 1 tablespoon butter in a skillet. Separate the onion slices into rings and add to the skillet. Sauté until golden brown. Drain on paper towels. Set aside.

Cut the French bread loaf in half. Hollow out each half, leaving the crusty shells intact. Reserve the soft bread for crumbs or other use.

Spread the inside of the half-loaves with mustard and mayonnaise. Spoon half of the poultry salad filling or seafood salad filling inside each hollow loaf section, and pack well. Then stuff each loaf half with the sautéed onions, pushing to pack well. Brush the surface of loaf sections with softened butter.

If a double-sided griddle is not available, place 1 loaf section on a griddle or in a skillet large enough to hold the bread. Heat another skillet and place the hot bottom directly over the loaf. Weight down with a heavy object or brick to flatten loaf slightly. Cook until bread is toasted or grilled on both sides. Cut each loaf section diagonally into 2-inch slices. Serve with French-fried potatoes and pickles, if desired.

MAKES 4 TO 6 SERVINGS

Poultry or Meat Salad Filling

1 cup diced cooked chicken, turkey, leftover roast or luncheon meat, or ham
¼ cup chopped pickles
¼ cup mayonnaise
½ cup chopped celery

Combine the chicken, pickles, mayonnaise, and celery. Mix well.

Seafood Salad Filling

1 cup flaked tuna, salmon, crab meat, or chopped shrimp
1 tablespoon lemon juice
¼ cup mayonnaise
½ cup chopped celery

Combine the tuna, lemon juice, mayonnaise, and celery. Mix well.

GRILLED GAME HENS

4 Cornish game hens
Salt and pepper to taste
⅓ cup dry white wine
¼ cup melted butter or margarine
Ripe black olives, pitted and halved
Lemon slices

Sprinkle the game hens inside and out with salt and pepper. Spear the hens on a rotisserie rod, arranging them tightly side by side to keep them rotating evenly. Tie together, if necessary. You may also add either a whole or half-lemon in the cavities before roasting.

Combine the wine and butter in a small bowl. Roast the game hens for about 1 hour and 15 minutes, or until done. Rotate them slowly, and baste them frequently with the wine-butter sauce. To cook the hens indoors, cook them on a rotisserie in a 350 degree oven.

Garnish with olives and lemon slices, and serve either warm or cold.

MAKES 4 SERVINGS

OPPOSITE, LEFT: *Duckling with Mole Sauce (page 128)*

CENTER: *Athenian Pizza (page 93); Wagon Wheel Pasta Salad (page 92); Grilled Game Hens (page 125)*

Orange Honeyed Chicken

3 whole chicken breasts, split
2 tablespoons butter or margarine
1/2 cup orange juice
2 tablespoons honey
2 tablespoons chopped onions
1/8 teaspoon black pepper
Salt
Hot cooked rice
2 tablespoons white wine or water
1 tablespoon flour
2 large oranges, peeled and sectioned (reserve the peel)
1 orange, sliced, for garnish
Parsley, for garnish
1 teaspoon grated orange peel or orange zest

In a large skillet brown the chicken in butter on both sides. Add the orange juice, honey, onions, pepper, and salt to taste. Cover and simmer for 20 minutes, or until chicken is tender. Remove chicken from pan and arrange over rice on a platter. Keep warm.

To prepare the sauce, stir the wine into the flour and blend well. Add to pan drippings and cook, stirring, until thickened. Add the orange sections and peel, and heat through. Spoon over the chicken. Garnish with orange slices and parsley.

MAKES 6 SERVINGS

Stir-Fried Chicken and Zucchini

2 whole chicken breasts, skinned, boned, and cut into thin strips
Pepper
2 tablespoons oil
2 tablespoons butter or margarine
1/4 teaspoon minced garlic
1 medium onion, sliced
3/4 pound zucchini, thinly sliced
1/2 pound mushrooms, sliced
1/2 cup shredded carrot
Grated peel and juice of 1/2 lemon
1/2 cup walnut halves
Hot cooked rice, optional

Season the chicken with pepper. In a large skillet stir-fry the chicken in oil until lightly browned and tender. Remove chicken from pan and set aside. Add butter to pan and stir-fry garlic and onion until onion is just tender. Add the zucchini, mushrooms, and carrot, and stir-fry over medium heat for 3 minutes. Add chicken and heat through. Stir in lemon peel and juice and walnut halves. Toss together to mix. Serve over hot rice, if desired.

MAKES 4 SERVINGS

Duckling with Mole Sauce

2 (4- to 5-pound) ducklings, quartered
Salt
1 cup chopped onion
1 clove garlic, minced
2 tablespoons oil
1/2 cup tomato sauce
1/4 cup raisins
1/4 cup creamy peanut butter
2 teaspoons sugar
1 teaspoon chili powder
1/4 teaspoon cinnamon
Dash ground cloves
1/2 ounce (1/2 square) unsweetened chocolate
1 1/2 cups water
1 chicken bouillon cube
Chopped peanuts, optional

Wash, drain, and dry the ducklings. Sprinkle both sides with salt. Place the duckling skin side up on a rack in a shallow roasting pan. Bake at 350 degrees until meat is tender, about 1 to 1 1/4 hours.

To prepare the mole sauce, sauté the onion and garlic in oil until tender but not brown. Combine the onion mixture, tomato sauce, raisins, peanut butter, sugar, chili powder, cinnamon, cloves, chocolate, water, and bouillon cube in a blender or in a food processor. Blend until smooth. Put the mixture in a saucepan, bring to a boil, reduce heat, and simmer for 15 to 20 minutes, stirring frequently. Brush sauce liberally over the ducklings at serving time; sprinkle with chopped peanuts. Or, serve the sauce and chopped peanuts on the side.

MAKES 4 TO 6 SERVINGS

ARROZ CON POLLO Á LA CUBANA

1 tablespoon oil
1 tablespoon lard
1 broiler-fryer, cut in serving pieces
1 small slice ham, chopped
1 smoked pork chop, boned and chopped
1½ green peppers, sliced lengthwise
½ pimiento, sliced lengthwise
1 small onion, peeled and chopped
1 clove garlic, minced
4 tomatoes, peeled and seeded
Salt, pepper
2 tablespoons sherry
4 cups water, or half water and half chicken stock
1½ cups rice
¼ teaspoon saffron
Additional pimiento, for garnish

Heat the oil and lard in a Dutch oven. Add the chicken and brown. Remove the chicken. Add the ham and pork chop. When brown, remove from skillet. Now add the green peppers, pimiento, onion, and garlic, and sauté until tender, adding more oil if needed. Add the chopped tomatoes, salt and pepper to taste, and sherry. Return the chicken, pork, and ham to the pot and cook for about 10 minutes.

Add water or part water and part stock. Add the rice and saffron. Stir, cover, and cook over medium heat until the rice is tender, about 45 minutes. Garnish with additional pimiento.

MAKES 4 TO 6 SERVINGS

MEAT

NARSAI'S POMEGRANATE LAMB
Janet Trefethen, Trefethen Vineyards

LAMB SHANKS
Musso & Frank Grill

BROCHETTES OF LAMB
Club Culinaire Français de Californie, Los Angeles

ROAST VEAL LOIN WITH SHALLOTS AND WILD
    MUSHROOM SAUCE
Gary Danko, Beringer Vineyards

VEAL PICCATA
Valentino

VEAL FILLET WITH GREEN PEPPERCORN SAUCE
Werner Albrecht, Five-Star Catering Co., Inc.

OSSO BUCO
Giuseppe Bellisario, Giuseppe!

ARISTA
Evan Kleiman and Viana La Place, Angeli

TENDERLOIN OF PORK KOBE-STYLE
John Ash, John Ash & Co., Santa Rosa

PEPPONE'S PORK SCALOPPINE
Pacific Dining Car

PORK DIJONNAISE
Au Relais, Sonoma

BRAISED SHORT RIBS
The Grill

PIMIENTO-WRAPPED ITALIAN SAUSAGES
Tutto Italia

MEATLOAF 72 MARKET STREET
Leonard Schwartz, 72 Market Street

RIS DE VEAU SOUS CLOCHE VIRGINIENNE
The Tower

FRIED LUMPIA

BUL-KOGI
(Korean Barbecue)

CROWN OF PORK WITH SAFFRON RICE STUFFING

ARTILLERY RACK OF LAMB

The rolling hills of Napa Valley are blanketed with vineyards and wineries that produce some of the finest cabernet sauvignons and chardonnays in the nation—if not the world. But wines are not the only outstanding feature of Napa Valley. Some of the finest hosts in America live and entertain at their vineyard estates, serving Lucullan repasts that feature products of the land around them. The centerpiece of their menus, whether formal dinners or sumptuous picnics, is frequently an elegant meat dish, often prepared with wine, always served with it. The Roast Veal Loin with Shallots and Wild Mushroom Sauce (page 132), served at a winemakers' picnic by Beringer winery chef Gary Danko, was accompanied by the winery's chardonnay, said to rival the great white Burgundies of France.

Although beef is still a favorite meat for various barbecue preparations—for example, Bul-Kogi, a Korean barbecue (page 141)—delicate white veal and young lamb are appealing more and more to the sophisticated diner. At Trefethen Vineyards, lamb marinated in pomegranate juice (page 132) is broiled over coals and served with their cabernet sauvignon for a memorable feast.

California entertaining takes place both indoors and outdoors, on the patios, terraces, and gardens that are an extension of the home. One still can manage to barbecue for an indoor meal simply by reaching out to the patio behind the kitchen door or by using a built-in kitchen grill.

Arista (page 134)

NARSAI'S POMEGRANATE LAMB
Janet Trefethen, Trefethen Vineyards

1 (5- to 6-pound) leg of lamb (bone-in)
1 cup unsweetened pomegranate juice
1/2 cup dry red wine
2 large onions
1 lemon, unpeeled, chopped
3 cloves garlic
1 teaspoon black pepper
1 tablespoon basil leaves
1 teaspoon salt

Have your butcher butterfly the leg of lamb, or do it yourself. In a blender combine the pomegranate juice, red wine, onions, lemon, garlic, pepper, basil, and salt. Rub marinade well into lamb.

Place the meat in a shallow glass or enamel pan. Pour remaining marinade over meat. Marinate in refrigerator overnight.

When ready to cook, wipe off excess marinade. Grill over medium coals, or roast the lamb in a 325 degree oven until thermometer reaches 145 degrees for medium-rare. Wait 5 to 10 minutes before carving.

MAKES ABOUT 10 SERVINGS

LAMB SHANKS
Musso & Frank Grill

4 lamb shanks
1 clove garlic, minced
Salt, pepper
8 medium carrots, peeled, and cut in chunks
8 small white onions, peeled
8 button mushrooms, caps only
8 small celery slices
1 (8-ounce) can tomato sauce
1 cup green peas

Sprinkle lamb shanks with garlic and season to taste with salt and pepper. Bake at 350 degrees for about 30 minutes, turning frequently to brown on all sides. Add the carrots, onions, mushrooms, celery, and tomato sauce. Raise heat to 375 degrees, add the peas, and continue to bake for 45 minutes to 1 hour, or until meat is tender. Add peas after 30 minutes cooking time.

MAKES 4 SERVINGS

BROCHETTES OF LAMB
Club Culinaire Français de Californie, Los Angeles

2 pounds boneless leg of lamb, cut into large cubes
2 onions, cut into squares
1 tablespoon chopped fresh rosemary
1 tablespoon chopped fresh tarragon
1 tablespoon chopped fresh parsley
Salt, pepper

Thread lamb cubes onto metal skewers alternately with onion squares. Place brochettes in a wide, shallow pan and sprinkle all over with rosemary, tarragon, and parsley, and season to taste with salt and pepper.

Heat coals on barbecue grill until hot. Add the brochettes and cook until done as desired, turning often to brown evenly.

MAKES 6 SERVINGS

ROAST VEAL LOIN WITH SHALLOTS AND WILD MUSHROOM SAUCE
Gary Danko, Beringer Vineyards

1/2 cup chopped parsley
4 cloves garlic, minced
2 tablespoons olive oil
1 (2-pound) boned and trimmed side of veal loin, tied
6 shallots, thinly sliced
3 1/2 cups veal stock or other meat stock
1 1/2 to 2 cups chardonnay
2 large shiitake mushrooms, stemmed and sliced
1 cup heavy cream
Salt, freshly cracked black pepper
1 tablespoon chopped mixed herbs (such as rosemary, thyme, basil, oregano, parsley)

Mix the parsley, garlic, and olive oil to make a paste. Rub entire surface of the veal roast with the garlic paste. Place on a rack in a roasting pan. Roast meat at 350 degrees for 1 hour, or until meat thermometer inserted in thickest part of roast registers 160° for rare or 170° for medium.

Meanwhile, combine the shallots with the veal stock and chardonnay in a skillet. Bring to a boil, and boil until liquid is reduced to a thick glaze in the pan. Add the shiitake mushrooms and cream. Bring back to a boil. Boil until slightly thickened or until sauce coats the back of a metal spoon. Season to taste with salt and pepper. Swirl in the herbs. Slice the meat and arrange on a platter. Pour the sauce over the meat slices.

MAKES 6 SERVINGS

VEAL PICCATA
Valentino

18 slices veal scallops, about 2 pounds
Flour
Cottonseed oil
2 tablespoons butter
Juice of 2 lemons
1/2 cup white wine
Chopped parsley
Salt, pepper
Lemon wedges

Pound the scallopine paper thin. Dip in flour and then sauté in the oil until browned, about 30 seconds. Remove veal, set aside, and keep warm. Drain the oil and add the butter and lemon juice. Add the wine and reduce the sauce by one-third. Add chopped parsley, salt, and pepper to taste. Spoon over the veal, and serve with lemon wedges.

MAKES 6 SERVINGS

VEAL FILLET WITH GREEN PEPPERCORN SAUCE
Werner Albrecht, Five-Star Catering Co., Inc.

2 small artichokes, cooked
4 small carrots, cut in 1-inch pieces
2 small turnips, cut in eighths
1 pound veal fillet, cut in 12 slices
1 cup red wine

3/4 cup strong veal or beef stock
3 tablespoons green peppercorns, drained
4 small green onions, diced
Salt

Halve the artichokes and remove any tough outer leaves and the chokes. If desired, shape the carrot and turnip pieces into a smaller version of the whole vegetable. Steam the carrots and turnips until tender-crisp. Keep warm.

Sauté the veal in a nonstick skillet just long enough to lightly brown on the outside; the inside should be pink. Add red wine and simmer for 8 minutes to reduce the liquid. Add veal stock, peppercorns, and green onions. Heat through. Season to taste with salt. Arrange the veal slices and vegetables on plate. Spoon the sauce over the meat.

MAKES 4 SERVINGS

OSSO BUCO
Giuseppe Bellisario, Giuseppe!

6 pounds veal shanks
1/4 cup flour
1/2 teaspoon salt
1/4 teaspoon black pepper
1/2 cup olive oil
1 medium onion, minced
1 medium carrot, minced
1 stalk celery, minced
2 cloves garlic, minced
1 cup dry white wine
1 cup beef broth
2 (1-pound 13-ounce) cans tomatoes, drained
1/2 teaspoon basil
1/2 teaspoon rosemary
Gremolata (recipe page 134)

Have the veal shanks cut into 2-inch pieces and secure them with string. Coat the shanks with flour seasoned with salt and pepper. Heat 1/4 cup olive oil in a heavy skillet. Add the shanks, a few pieces at a time, and brown well on all sides.

While the veal is browning, sauté the onion, carrot, celery, and garlic in remaining 1/4 cup oil in a large casserole or Dutch oven. Cook, stirring occasionally, until vegetables are tender.

When the veal is browned, arrange on top of the vegetables. Place the wine, beef broth, tomatoes, basil, and rosemary in the pan used to brown the veal and cook, stirring to loosen any bits and pieces of meat that may have stuck to the pan. Bring to a boil, and incorporate the scrapings from the bottom of the pan, then pour the sauce over the veal. Cover casserole. Bake at 350 degrees for 1½ hours or until veal is very tender.

Remove veal to a warm platter, and cut away the strings. Spoon off fat from the pan juices, and ladle the juice over the veal. Sprinkle with gremolata and serve with rice or pasta.

MAKES 6 TO 8 SERVINGS

Note: Veal shanks may be purchased or ordered at gourmet meat markets.

Gremolata

6 cloves garlic, minced
2 tablespoons grated lemon peel
½ cup chopped parsley

Mix the garlic, lemon peel, and parsley.

Arista
Evan Kleiman and Viana La Place, Angeli

6 cloves garlic, minced
1 to 2 tablespoons fennel seeds
2 teaspoons coarse salt
Freshly ground pepper
1 (7-pound) boneless pork rib roast
Fruity olive oil

Make a paste of minced garlic, fennel seeds, and salt and pepper to taste in a mortar and pestle, or mash with the side of a chef's knife. Unroll roast, if tied. Spread most of the paste over the meat, reserving 1 tablespoon or more. Roll and tie roast so that the white tenderloin is in the center and dark meat is on the outside. Make a few incisions with a sharp knife about ½-inch deep in roast and stuff with some of the paste. Rub olive oil over meat and place in roasting pan.

Roast, uncovered, at 350 degrees for 2½ to 3 hours or until thermometer inserted in center registers 170 degrees. Baste the roast 2 or 3 times with pan juices. Remove roast from oven and cool slightly. Slice into ½-inch slices and drizzle olive oil over meat, if desired.

MAKES 8 TO 10 SERVINGS

Tenderloin of Pork Kobe-Style
John Ash, John Ash & Co., Santa Rosa

2 (1-pound) tenderloins of pork (fat and silver skin removed)
½ cup soy sauce
1 (3-inch) piece fresh ginger root, mashed
Grated peel and juice of 1 orange
2 cloves garlic, mashed
¼ cup honey
¼ cup sesame seeds
Mirin Sauce (recipe follows)
Orange segments (or kumquats), for garnish
⅓ Japanese radish (daikon) shredded into threads

Place the pork fillet in a shallow pan. Combine the soy sauce, ginger, orange peel and juice, and garlic in a small bowl. Pour over the pork. Turn to coat well. Remove fillet from marinade. Roll in honey and sprinkle sesame seeds to cover the surface of the pork. Place on a rack over a roasting pan and roast at 475 degrees until meat thermometer registers 160 degrees for medium rare or 170 degrees for well done, about 30 minutes. Slice and garnish with orange segments or kumquats, and daikon threads. Serve with mirin sauce.

SERVES 6 TO 8

Mirin Sauce

½ cup mirin (sweet sake)
½ cup fermented Japanese soy sauce
½ cup chicken stock
2 tablespoons sugar
1 (1-inch) piece ginger root, sliced (do not peel)
1 clove garlic, mashed
1 star anise pod
Juice of 1 large orange
1 tablespoon cornstarch
Water

Combine mirin, soy sauce, chicken stock, sugar, ginger root, garlic, anise pod, and orange juice in a saucepan. Mix cornstarch with enough water to make a thin paste. Stir into mirin mixture. Bring to a simmer. Simmer over medium-low heat until sauce thickens and becomes shiny. Strain.

MAKES ABOUT 1¾ CUPS

ABOVE: *Narsai's Pomegranate Lamb*
(page 132)

RIGHT: *Veal Fillet with Green Peppercorn*
Sauce (page 133)

PEPPONE'S PORK SCALOPPINE
Pacific Dining Car

¼ cup butter plus 1 tablespoon
3 pounds pork loin scallops (about 16 scallops)
3 tablespoons minced garlic
2 red peppers, cut in strips
2 green peppers, cut in strips
1½ pounds mushrooms, sliced
1 tablespoon dried rosemary
3 tablespoons lemon juice
½ cup beef broth
Dash Worcestershire sauce
Salt, pepper

Melt ¼ cup butter in a large skillet. Add the pork and cook until browned on both sides. Drain off excess fat from pan. Add the garlic, red and green peppers, mushrooms, and rosemary. Sauté 2 minutes, stirring constantly. Add lemon juice and beef broth. Stir 1 minute. Add Worcestershire and season to taste with salt and pepper. Add 1 tablespoon butter and stir until melted.

MAKES 8 SERVINGS

PORK DIJONNAISE
Au Relais, Sonoma

6 medium pork chops
2 tablespoons butter or margarine
2 shallots, chopped
2 cloves garlic, chopped
12 cornichons, julienne-cut
½ cup dry white wine
½ cup heavy cream
2 tablespoons Dijon mustard
Chopped parsley or cilantro, for garnish

In a large skillet sauté the pork chops in 1½ tablespoons butter until browned and almost done. Place in a baking dish and bake, covered, at 350 degrees for 15 minutes, or until meat is well done. Remove meat and keep warm. Drain off excess fat.

Add remaining ½ tablespoon butter to pan and melt. Add shallots and garlic, and sauté 10 seconds. Add cornichons and wine. Bring to a simmer and simmer over medium-high heat

until glaze is formed. Stir in the cream and Dijon mustard. Cook and stir until heated through and smooth.

Place pork on serving dish. Pour sauce over meat. Serve sprinkled with chopped parsley.

MAKES 6 SERVINGS

BRAISED SHORT RIBS
The Grill

Oil
2½ pounds kosher-cut short ribs
1 cup combined cubed onion, celery, carrots
1 bay leaf
¼ cup brandy
2 cups beef stock
1 tablespoon arrowroot
Salt, pepper
1 onion, cut into 3-inch julienne pieces
1 turnip, peeled and cut into 3-inch julienne pieces
Chopped parsley, for garnish

Heat 2 tablespoons oil in a large skillet. Add the short ribs and sauté for 2 minutes on each side or until browned. Remove from pan. Set aside. Add another 2 tablespoons oil to the skillet and heat. Add the cubed vegetables and bay leaf and sauté for 5 minutes or until browned.

Place the braised vegetables and short ribs in a roasting pan. Bake at 450 degrees for 15 to 20 minutes to braise. Add brandy and beef stock. Reduce oven heat to 350 degrees and bake, covered, for 1 hour and 45 minutes to 2 hours, or until meat falls away from bone. Remove short ribs from pan and set aside. Discard cubed vegetables.

Strain the liquid in which the meat cooked. Melt 1 tablespoon oil in a small skillet. Stir in the arrowroot until smooth. Cook and stir until golden brown. Stir in ½ cup strained liquid until well blended. Cook, stirring until smooth and slightly thickened. Gradually add remaining strained liquid and continue cooking over medium-low heat, stirring until the sauce is smooth and slightly thickened. Strain again. Season to taste with salt and pepper.

Heat 1 to 2 tablespoons oil. Add the julienned onion and turnip and sauté until lightly browned. Place the julienned vegetables on the short ribs, and pour the sauce over the vegetables. Garnish with parsley.

MAKES 4 TO 6 SERVINGS

PIMIENTO-WRAPPED ITALIAN SAUSAGES
Tutto Italia

8 hot Italian sausages
Juice of 1 lemon
1/4 teaspoon crushed red pepper flakes
8 pieces canned pimiento or sweet red pepper
1 tablespoon red wine vinegar
1/4 teaspoon oregano
Salt, pepper
Chopped green onions, for garnish

Place the sausages in a baking dish. Sprinkle with half the lemon juice and all of the crushed red pepper flakes. Bake at 375 degrees for about 1 hour or until sausages are browned and crispy. Drain.

Wrap each sausage with red pepper. Place seam side down on a serving platter. Combine remaining lemon juice, red wine vinegar, and oregano in a small bowl. Season to taste with salt and pepper. Mix well and pour over the sausages. Garnish with chopped green onions.

MAKES 8 SERVINGS

MEATLOAF 72 MARKET STREET
Leonard Schwartz, 72 Market Street

3/4 cup minced onion
3/4 cup minced green onion
1/2 cup minced celery
1/2 cup minced carrot
1/4 cup minced green pepper
1/4 cup minced red pepper
2 teaspoons minced garlic
3 tablespoons butter
1 teaspoon salt
1/4 teaspoon cayenne pepper
1 teaspoon black pepper
1/2 teaspoon white pepper
1/2 teaspoon ground cumin
1/2 teaspoon nutmeg

1/2 cup half and half
1/2 cup catsup
1 1/2 pounds lean ground beef
1/2 pound lean ground pork
3 eggs, beaten
3/4 cup dry bread crumbs
Gravy (recipe follows)

Sauté the onion, green onion, celery, carrot, green pepper, red pepper, and garlic in the butter until the vegetables are soft. Remove from skillet to a large bowl. Add the salt, cayenne, black and white pepper, cumin, and nutmeg to the vegetable mixture. Stir in the half and half, catsup, beef, pork, eggs, and bread crumbs. Mix well. Form into a loaf and place on a greased baking dish. Bake at 350 degrees for 45 to 50 minutes. Let stand 10 minutes before slicing. Pour off excess fat. Slice and serve with gravy.

MAKES 6 TO 8 SERVINGS

Gravy

4 shallots, minced
2 tablespoons butter
1 sprig thyme
1 bay leaf
Pinch crushed black pepper
1 cup dry white wine
1 cup veal or beef stock
1 cup chicken stock
Salt, pepper

Sauté the shallots in 1 tablespoon butter with the thyme, bay leaf, and black pepper. Add white wine and simmer over high heat until reduced to a glaze. Add the veal stock and the chicken stock, and simmer over high heat until sauce is reduced by one-third to one-half. Stir in remaining 1 tablespoon butter, and salt and pepper to taste until butter melts. Discard thyme sprig and bay leaf. Serve with the meat loaf.

MAKES 1 CUP

*Co-owner Bob Spivak with a chef, John Sola, at
The Grill*

Braised Short Ribs (page 136)

John Ash
Tenderloin of Pork Kobe-Style (page 134)

RIS DE VEAU SOUS CLOCHE VIRGINIENNE
The Tower

4 pounds sweetbreads
Salt, pepper
Flour
6 tablespoons butter
2 tablespoons oil
6 slices white bread
6 mushroom caps
6 slices Virginia ham
Quick Demi-Glace (recipe follows)

Soak the sweetbreads in cold water for 24 hours, changing the water several times.

The next day, place the sweetbreads in a saucepan and cover with water. Bring to simmer and simmer, uncovered, 15 minutes. Drain and plunge into cold water. Let stand 5 minutes, then drain again.

Remove any gristle and skin from the sweetbreads. Cut each sweetbread into 3 slices. Season to taste with salt and pepper and dredge in flour. Sauté in 2 tablespoons butter and 2 tablespoons oil until golden brown. In a separate skillet sauté the bread in 2 tablespoons butter until golden on both sides. Next, sauté the mushrooms in another 2 tablespoons butter. Place a slice of ham on each piece of fried bread. Cover with sweetbreads and top with a mushroom cap. Serve with the demi-glace on the side.

MAKES 6 SERVINGS

Quick Demi-Glace

4 cups beef consommé
¼ cup Marsala wine
4 teaspoons cornstarch
1½ tablespoons water

Reduce the consommé to 2 cups over high heat. Lower heat until liquid is at a simmer. Stir in the Marsala. Combine the cornstarch and water until smooth, and stir into the consommé. Simmer until mixture is smooth and has thickened.

MAKES 2 CUPS

FRIED LUMPIA

½ pound ground pork
½ pound uncooked shrimp, finely chopped
½ cup minced mushrooms
½ cup diced peeled jicama
2 green onions, finely chopped
3 egg yolks
2 tablespoons soy sauce
Lumpia wrappers
Oil for deep-frying
Sweet-Sour Sauce (recipe follows) or catsup

Mix the pork, shrimp, mushrooms, jicama, green onions, egg yolks, and soy sauce in a bowl. Mix well. Shape about 1½ tablespoons meat mixture into a strip, and place along one side of a lumpia wrapper. Roll tightly, folding in the ends while rolling. Moisten edges lightly with water to seal. Fry in deep hot oil until golden brown. Serve whole or cut in halves or thirds. Serve with sweet-sour sauce.

MAKES ABOUT 6 SERVINGS

Note: Lumpia wrappers (eggroll skins) are available in Chinese markets.

Sweet-Sour Sauce

¼ cup cider vinegar
1 teaspoon soy sauce
½ cup sugar
1 cup water or pineapple juice
½ teaspoon finely grated ginger root
½ clove garlic, crushed
2 tablespoons cornstarch, blended with 2 tablespoons cold water
Salt

Combine the vinegar, soy sauce, sugar, water, ginger, and garlic in a small saucepan. Bring to a boil. Stir in cornstarch paste and simmer 5 minutes, or until thickened. Season to taste with salt.

MAKES 1⅔ CUPS

BUL-KOGI
(Korean Barbecue)

Pork Barbecue

1 pound lean pork
1 1/2 teaspoons red pepper paste or pinch of red pepper
2 1/2 tablespoons sugar
4 1/2 tablespoons soy sauce
4 tablespoons minced green onions
1 1/2 teaspoons minced ginger root
2 1/2 teaspoons minced garlic
2 tablespoons ground sesame seeds
Pinch pepper
2 tablespoons sesame seed oil

Cut the pork into cubes. Stir the paste into the pork cubes to coat. Sprinkle with sugar. Add soy sauce, green onions, ginger, garlic, sesame seeds, pepper, and sesame seed oil. Marinate 30 minutes to blend flavors.

Wrap in foil and bake at 350 degrees for about 50 minutes or until the pork cubes are tender. If desired, broil the pork on a rack 4 inches from heat source, turning and basting them, for about 30 minutes.

MAKES 4 TO 6 SERVINGS

Beef Barbecue

1 pound lean beef
2 1/2 tablespoons sugar
4 1/2 tablespoons soy sauce
4 tablespoons minced green onions
2 1/2 teaspoons minced garlic
1 1/2 teaspoons minced ginger root
2 tablespoons ground sesame seeds
2 tablespoons sesame seed oil

Sprinkle the beef with sugar. Add soy sauce, green onions, garlic, ginger, and sesame seeds. Marinate 30 minutes to blend flavors. Toss with oil.

Wrap in foil and bake at 350 degrees for about 50 minutes or until the meat is tender. Or, place the foil packet over medium coals on an hibachi and grill for 30 minutes. Meat may also be broiled about 3 inches from heat source until done as desired, turning and basting occasionally.

MAKES 4 TO 6 SERVINGS

Chicken Barbecue

2 chicken breasts, skinned and boned
1 1/2 teaspoons sugar
4 tablespoons minced green onions
2 teaspoons minced garlic
1 teaspoon minced ginger root
2 tablespoons ground sesame seeds
Pinch pepper
4 tablespoons soy sauce
2 tablespoons sesame seed oil

Cut the chicken into flat slices, sprinkle with sugar, then add the onions, garlic, ginger, sesame seeds, pepper, and soy sauce. Marinate 30 minutes to blend flavors. Toss chicken with sesame seed oil.

Wrap the chicken in foil and bake at 350 degrees for 40 minutes, or place over medium coals on an hibachi and cook 30 minutes.

MAKES 4 TO 6 SERVINGS

CROWN OF PORK WITH SAFFRON RICE STUFFING

2 (7- to 9-rib) pork loin roasts
Saffron Rice Stuffing (recipe page 143)

Have the butcher prepare and tie pork roasts into a crown roast. Remove the pork from the refrigerator 1 hour before roasting. Wipe with a damp cloth and cover the bones with aluminum foil. Place in a 350-degree oven and immediately reduce temperature to 325 degrees. Bake 30 minutes per pound, about 3 1/2 hours in all, or until 160° on a meat thermometer. Remove the roast from the oven 30 to 40 minutes before it is done and fill the center with saffron rice stuffing. Return to oven and complete cooking.

MAKES 10 TO 12 SERVINGS

Crown of Pork with Saffron Rice (page 141)

Saffron Rice Stuffing

4¹/₂ cups chicken broth
4 tablespoons butter
¹/₄ teaspoon powdered saffron
2 cups long-grain rice
1 (6-ounce) package dried apricots, cut in slivers
1 cup thinly sliced celery
1 cup halved pecans

In a Dutch oven combine the chicken broth, 2 tablespoons butter, and saffron. Cover, and bring to a boil. Stir in the rice. Cover tightly and cook 15 minutes. Uncover and quickly stir in the apricots. Cover tightly again and cook 5 minutes or until all the chicken broth has been absorbed. Meanwhile, melt remaining butter in a skillet. Add the celery and pecans and sauté 3 minutes, or until celery is tender and pecans golden. Remove rice from heat; stir in celery mixture. Cover and refrigerate until ready to use. Use to fill center cavity of roast, but do not pack firmly. Spoon remaining stuffing into lightly greased baking pan. Cover with foil and place in oven with roast.

ARTILLERY RACK OF LAMB

2 (3¹/₂- to 4-pound) racks of lamb with 8 to 9 chops each
2 to 3 cloves garlic, split
Salt, pepper
Crushed, dried rosemary

Have the butcher "French" the bone ends of racks. Rub each rack generously with garlic and season lightly with salt, pepper, and rosemary. Cover exposed bone tips with small pieces of foil.

Place the lamb roasts on racks in shallow baking pans and roast at 325 to 400 degrees until thermometer placed in thickest part of chops registers 140 degrees for medium rare, 160 degrees for medium, or 170 degrees for well done.

Remove roasts from the oven and place the bone sides together, intertwining the ends of the rib bones so they resemble stacked rifles. Discard foil and cover bone tips with paper frills, if desired. Allow to stand 10 minutes before carving.

MAKES ABOUT 8 SERVINGS OF 2 CHOPS EACH

Artillery Rack of Lamb (recipe this page)

SWEET THINGS

SUMMER FRUIT WITH FROMAGE BLANC
Laura Chenel and Linda Siegfried

PAULINE'S BLACKBERRY ICE CREAM
Janet Trefethen, Trefethen Vineyards

SANTA ROSA PLUM ICE CREAM
Janet Trefethen, Trefethen Vineyards

FRENCH FRUIT TARTS
Michel Richard

ALMOND TART WITH LEMON CURD
Gary Danko, Beringer Vineyards

PECAN TARTS
Spago

NEON TUMBLEWEED WITH CACTUS COOKIES
John Sedlar, St. Estèphe

UDO'S ALMOND TILE COOKIES
Janet Trefethen, Trefethen Vineyards

HOLIDAY CHARLOTTE
Le Petit Four

GÂTEAU ST. HONORÉ
Mary Sue Milliken and Susan Feniger,
    City restaurant

MONTMARTRE
Michel Richard

WHITE MOUSSE CAKE WITH ZEST OF GRAPEFRUIT
    AND PINE NUTS
John Sedlar, St. Estèphe

LA MORT AU CHOCOLAT
(Chocolate Death)
Les Anges

IL NIDO DOLCE
(The Sweet Nest)
Pasta Etc.

WALNUT BREAD
Rancho Bernardo Inn, San Diego

SEED BREAD
Katie Trefethen, Trefethen Vineyards

FRESH LEMON ICE

RASPBERRY ICE

PINEAPPLE SORBET

CALIFORNIA FRUIT TERRINE

PEARS AND CREAM CHEESE

CRANBERRY-ORANGE TART

ZUCCHINI BREAD

VANILLA SOUFFLÉ

You will understand why it is easy for Californians to love desserts when you look at the sweet things in this chapter. They are irresistible, and among the highlights of California cuisine. We asked several of the rising restaurant chefs in Los Angeles to share a favorite festive dessert and here are some of their prize recipes.

The chef at Le Petit Four gave us his directions for Holiday Charlotte (page 152), a chilled chocolate dessert topped with colorful fruit. Mary Sue Milliken and Susan Feniger came up with a Gâteau St. Honoré (page 152) as they serve it at their popular City restaurant, and John Sedlar of St. Estèphe positively dazzled us with a white Christmas cake made of white chocolate mousse and covered with curls of white chocolate (page 153). Los Angeles pastry king Michel Richard, famed for his low calorie desserts, is represented by his fabulous Montmartre (page 153), while the wine country's entry is Summer Fruit with Fromage Blanc (page 145), a delicate dessert by Laura Chenel who blends one of her fresh, light goat cheeses, with California fruits and walnuts for an ethereal treat.

A gourmet deli called Pasta Etc. had a dessert called Il Nido Dolce (page 156) that swept us off our feet. Imagine chocolate-flavored pasta! Well, the pastry chef has created a nest of chocolate pasta cradling chocolate eggs filled with pastry cream. That may be the last word in new California cuisine.

SUMMER FRUIT WITH FROMAGE BLANC
Laura Chenel and Linda Siegfried

6 peaches
1½ cups fresh blackberries
Sugar (or honey)
2 tablespoons brandy
8 ounces (1 cup) soft chèvre (fromage blanc)
½ teaspoon grated lemon peel
¼ teaspoon vanilla extract
2 egg whites
Pinch salt
¼ cup ground walnuts, toasted

Peel and thinly slice peaches. Sort and pick through blackberries. Toss fruits in a bowl with 2 tablespoons sugar or honey, and the brandy. Let stand at room temperature for 1 hour.

Mix together the chèvre, lemon peel, vanilla, and ¼ cup sugar. Beat egg whites with 1 teaspoon sugar and salt until stiff. Gently fold beaten egg whites into cheese mixture. Divide fruit into 6 dessert dishes. Top each with some of the cheese mixture. Sprinkle with walnuts.

MAKES 6 SERVINGS

PAULINE'S BLACKBERRY ICE CREAM
Janet Trefethen, Trefethen Vineyards

¾ cup superfine sugar
3 to 4 cups blackberries
2 cups half and half

Place the sugar, blackberries, and half and half in a blender or food processor. Purée mixture. Pass through a sieve. Turn into an ice cream freezer canister, and freeze according to manufacturer's directions.

MAKES 10 TO 12 SERVINGS

SANTA ROSA PLUM ICE CREAM
Janet Trefethen, Trefethen Vineyards

¾ cup superfine sugar, or to taste (depending on sweetness of fruit)
1 quart chopped and pitted Santa Rosa plums
2 cups half and half

Place the sugar, plums, and half and half in a blender or processor. Purée. Turn into ice cream freezer canister, and freeze according to manufacturer's directions.

MAKES 10 TO 12 SERVINGS

FRENCH FRUIT TARTS
Michel Richard

1 pound cake flour
1¼ cups unsalted butter
1¼ cups brown sugar, packed
2 eggs, lightly beaten
1 cup ground hazelnuts
Hazelnut Cream (recipe page 148)
Sliced kiwi, strawberries, grapes, pineapple, or other seasonal fruit

Mix half the cake flour with the butter, sugar, eggs, and hazelnuts. Mix well. Add remaining flour. Mix lightly; do not overmix. Cover dough with plastic wrap and chill thoroughly.

Roll dough ⅛-inch thick. Using the rim of a 3½- to 4-inch tart pan as a guide, cut out dough circles. Fit, stretching dough slightly, into ten 3½- to 4-inch tart pans. Crimp edges and pierce dough lightly with fork tines.

Fill three-fourths full with hazelnut cream. Place the tarts on a clean baking sheet and bake at 350 degrees for 25 minutes, or until cream is set. Cool, then chill thoroughly.

Top each tart with an assortment of cut or sliced kiwi, strawberries, grapes, pineapple, or other seasonal fruit.

MAKES 10 TARTS

TOP: *California Fruit Terrine (page 160)*

RIGHT: *Michel Richard with tray of his Fruit Tarts (page 145)*

Hazelnut Cream

½ cup plus 2 tablespoons unsalted butter, at room
   temperature
¾ cup brown sugar
1 cup ground hazelnuts
2 small eggs
Juice of ½ lemon
Pastry Cream (recipe follows)

Beat the butter, brown sugar, hazelnuts, eggs (one at a time), and lemon juice. Blend well. Fold in the pastry cream, lightly but thoroughly.

Pastry Cream

3 egg yolks
2 tablespoons cornstarch
¼ cup sugar
Pinch salt
1 cup milk
½ vanilla bean, split

In a bowl beat the egg yolks with cornstarch, sugar, and salt until well blended. Heat the milk with the vanilla bean in a saucepan. Bring to a boil. Remove milk from heat. Remove vanilla bean. Using the tip of a knife, remove the seeds from the bean and return the seeds to the hot milk. Discard bean stems. Mix a small amount of the hot milk into the egg-sugar mixture. Return to the pan of hot milk, and stir to blend well. Bring to a boil. Remove from heat and cool until ready to use.

ALMOND TART WITH LEMON CURD
Gary Danko, Beringer Vineyards

¼ cup finely chopped almonds
1¼ cups flour, sifted
½ cup sugar
Pinch salt
½ cup butter, cut into ½-inch cubes
1 egg
1 teaspoon vanilla extract
Lemon Curd (recipe follows)
Sweetened whipped cream, for garnish
Fresh fruit, for garnish

Combine the almonds, flour, sugar, and salt in a bowl. Add the butter, bit by bit, rubbing into the flour by hand. Stir in the egg and vanilla to form a ball. Chill. Roll out onto 12-inch tart pan with removable bottom. Weight down with beans placed on wax paper.

    Bake at 350 degrees until golden, about 20 minutes. Cool. Pour lemon curd filling into cooled pie shell. Chill until set. Remove sides of pan. Garnish with whipped cream and cut-up fruit.

MAKES ONE 12-INCH TART

Lemon Curd

10 egg yolks
¾ to 1 cup sugar
¾ cup lemon juice
½ cup butter

Mix egg yolks, sugar, and lemon juice in the top of a double boiler. Cook, stirring constantly over simmering water, until mixture coats the back of a metal spoon. Do not allow to boil. Remove from heat and whisk in butter, bit by bit, until melted and smooth.

PECAN TARTS
Spago

1½ cups light corn syrup
¾ cup granulated sugar
¾ cup light brown sugar, packed
4 eggs plus 2 egg yolks
3 tablespoons unsalted butter
Tart Shells (recipe follows)
1½ to 2 cups unbroken pecan halves (6 to 8 ounces)
Caramel Sauce (recipe follows)

Combine the corn syrup, granulated and brown sugars, eggs, and egg yolks in a medium bowl. Stir until blended. Heat the butter in a small skillet over medium heat until the butter is foamy and light brown in color. Remove from heat and whisk into the corn syrup mixture. Set aside.

    Set the pastry-lined tart pans on a large baking sheet. Arrange the pecans among the tart pans and pour filling over them, or pour in the filling, and arrange the pecans on top in a symmetrical pattern. Bake at 375 degrees for 35 to 40 minutes. Remove to a wire rack to cool. Serve the tarts at room temperature topped with caramel sauce.

MAKES 6 TO 8 TARTS

Tart Shells

3 cups pastry flour
1 cup unsalted butter, very cold, cut into ½-inch pieces
3 tablespoons sugar
Pinch salt
2 egg yolks
1 to 2 tablespoons heavy cream, very cold

Place the flour, butter, sugar, and salt in a food processor. Process, using a quick on and off motion, until mixture resembles coarse meal. Combine egg yolks and 1 tablespoon cream in a small bowl. With the motor running, add the egg mixture. Process just until dough begins to form. Add enough remaining cream to form a dough that holds together. Scrape the dough onto a piece of foil. Wrap airtight and refrigerate until well chilled, at least 1 hour.

Divide the dough into 6 or 8 equal portions, depending on whether pan size is 3 or 4 inches. Roll each portion out onto a lightly floured pastry cloth. Carefully transfer the pastry to tart pans. Press against bottoms and sides of pans, then trim excess around the rims. If the pastry tears, patch with small bits of pastry trimmings. Reserve any remaining pastry, wrapped airtight, for another use. Refrigerate pastry-lined tart pans until ready to use.

MAKES 6 TO 8 SHELLS

Caramel Sauce

½ cup sugar, preferably vanilla sugar
⅔ cup heavy cream, at room temperature
2 tablespoons unsalted butter, at room temperature

Heat the sugar in a small, heavy skillet or saucepan over medium heat until melted and medium amber in color. Carefully pour in the cream all at once, being careful to avoid splatters. Stir in the butter. Cook, stirring constantly, over medium heat until caramel dissolves and sauce is smooth. Remove from heat. Store at room temperature if not using immediately, as sauce will harden if refrigerated.

MAKES ABOUT 1 CUP

NEON TUMBLEWEED WITH CACTUS COOKIES
John Sedlar, St. Estèphe

2 cups fresh raspberries
2 cups fresh blackberries
6 kiwis
1 papaya
¼ cup lemon juice
¼ cup sugar
Banana
Pineapple
Whole Raspberries
Cactus Cookies (recipe follows)

Purée raspberries, blackberries, kiwis, and papaya separately in a blender or food processor, adding 1 tablespoon lemon juice and 1 tablespoon sugar as each fruit is fully blended. To make the tumbleweed, transfer puréed mixture to individual squeeze bottles and make erratic patterns on a plate. Cut remaining fruit into geometric shapes and place randomly on the tumbleweed. Serve with cactus cookies.

Cactus Cookies

1 cup butter, at room temperature
1½ cups sugar
2 eggs
½ teaspoon vanilla extract
1 teaspoon brandy
1½ teaspoons anise seed
1½ cups flour
1 teaspoon baking powder
Sugar
Cinnamon

Cream together the butter and sugar until light. Add the eggs, vanilla, brandy, anise seed, flour, and baking powder. Mix until well blended. Chill dough several hours.

Roll out dough to ¼-inch thickness. Cut into 2-inch cactus shapes. (Cactus cookie cutters are available in gourmet cookware shops.) Sprinkle cookies with sugar and cinnamon and bake at 375 degrees for about 10 minutes, or until lightly browned.

MAKES ABOUT 58 COOKIES

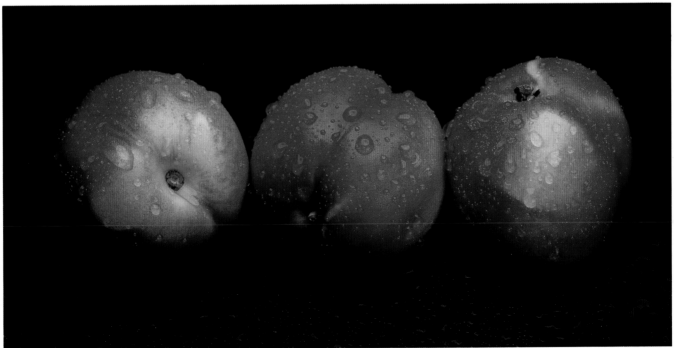

OPPOSITE: *Holiday Charlotte (page 152)*

Udo's Almond Tile Cookies
Janet Trefethen, Trefethen Vineyards

1 cup plus 5 teaspoons sugar
½ cup flour
6 egg whites
½ teaspoon vanilla extract
2 tablespoons butter or margarine, melted
1⅔ cup sliced almonds

Combine the sugar, flour, and egg whites. Stir to blend. Add the vanilla and melted butter. Gently fold in almonds. Drop mixture by the tablespoon, about 7 inches apart, onto a buttered baking sheet. With a fork dipped in water, spread batter to make 3-inch circles.

Bake at 350 degrees for 10 minutes. Remove the cookies from the baking sheet with a spatula and drape over rolling pin for a rounded effect. Repeat until all the batter has been used.

MAKES ABOUT 2 DOZEN COOKIES

Note: Do not attempt to make these cookies on high humidity days as they'll not turn out crisp.

Holiday Charlotte
Le Petit Four

1 (3-ounce) package ladyfingers
1 cup sugar
½ cup water
8 egg yolks
1 pound dark chocolate, melted
1 cup heavy cream, whipped
Fresh cut peaches, apricots, pears, strawberries,
  raspberries, papaya, and kiwi (canned fruit may be used)
¼ cup apple jelly, melted

Separate the ladyfingers and line the bottom and sides of a 9-inch charlotte mold or a bowl. Combine the sugar and water in a small saucepan. Bring to a boil. Boil 2 minutes. Cool.

Beat the egg yolks in a large bowl. Gradually beat in the sugar syrup. Add the melted chocolate. Fold in the whipped cream. Turn into the ladyfinger-lined pan, to within 1 inch of rim. Chill until set.

When ready to serve, remove the cake from the mold. Fill the top of the cake with fruit, then brush the fruit with melted apple jelly.

MAKES ONE 9-INCH CAKE

Gâteau St. Honoré
Mary Sue Milliken and Susan Feniger, City restaurant

1 pound puff pastry
2 cups sugar
16 cream puffs filled with pastry cream
Chocolate Filling (recipe follows)
2 cups heavy cream
3 ounces semisweet chocolate, melted

Roll the puff pastry into a 12-inch circle about ¼-inch thick. Pierce with a fork. Let rest 25 minutes. Place on a baking sheet, and bake at 450 degrees until golden brown, about 15 to 20 minutes.

Caramelize the sugar in an aluminum skillet until it turns golden brown. Do not overbrown. Remove immediately from heat. Using a fork, quickly dip one half of each cream puff into the caramel and place on buttered parchment paper. When the caramel has set, dip the uncoated half in the caramel. Cool.

Place the caramel-coated cream puffs around the puff pastry. Fill with the chilled chocolate filling. Whip the cream until soft peaks form. Fold melted chocolate into half of the whipped cream. Set aside. Spoon remaining half of whipped cream into a pastry bag fitted with a large round tube. Pipe dome-shaped balls in rows over the chocolate filling, leaving spaces between the rows. Repeat, using the chocolate whipped cream, filling in the spaces between the rows of white whipped cream.

MAKES ONE 12-INCH CAKE

Chocolate Filling

3 tablespoons brandy
½ cup golden raisins
9 ounces semisweet chocolate
7 ounces unsalted butter
5 eggs, separated

To plump the raisins, heat the brandy and raisins over low heat. Set aside to soak. Chop the chocolate into small pieces. Melt with the butter in the top of a double boiler over barely simmering water. When melted, remove immediately and whisk in the egg yolks. Add the plumped raisins. Beat the egg whites until soft peaks form. Fold into the chocolate-raisin mixture. Cover, and chill 3 to 4 hours or overnight.

Montmartre
Michel Richard

1 8-inch génoise or sponge cake layer, sliced into 2 layers
Raspberry-flavored liqueur
Sour Cream-Yogurt Filling (recipe follows)
1 10-ounce jar raspberry jelly, melted
2 pints fresh raspberries
2 cups heavy cream
2 tablespoons sugar

Generously butter an 8-inch springform pan. Cut a sheet of foil long enough to completely encircle the inside of the pan with a ½-inch overlap. Trim to 8 inches wide and fold in half lengthwise, and line the insides of the pan. Place 1 layer of the génoise in the pan. Brush generously with raspberry-flavored liqueur. Spread the sour cream-yogurt filling on top.

Top with the second cake layer. Brush with liqueur. Cover with plastic wrap and refrigerate several hours or overnight. Remove springform and foil and transfer the cake to a serving platter.

Smooth the edges of the cake with a spatula. Lightly brush the top with raspberry jelly. Arrange the raspberries on top. Whip the cream until soft peaks form. Gradually add sugar, beating until the cream is stiff. Reserve ⅓ cup for decoration. Spread the sweetened whipped cream around the sides of the cake. Pipe reserved whipped cream around edge of cake.

MAKES ONE 8-INCH CAKE

Sour Cream-Yogurt Filling

3 tablespoons frozen orange juice concentrate, thawed
1 envelope unflavored gelatin
4 egg yolks
¾ cup plus 2 tablespoons sugar
1 cup sour cream
½ cup plain low-fat yogurt
3 tablespoons Grand Marnier
1½ cups heavy cream

Mix the orange juice concentrate with 1 tablespoon water. Stir in gelatin to soften. Heat over low heat until gelatin is dissolved, stirring frequently. Cool slightly.

Beat egg yolks with ¾ cup sugar until light. Fold in the sour cream, yogurt, gelatin mixture, and Grand Marnier. Chill until slightly thickened. In another bowl beat the cream until soft peaks form. Gradually add remaining 2 tablespoons sugar, beating until stiff peaks form. Fold into yogurt mixture.

White Mousse Cake with Zest of Grapefruit and Pine Nuts
John Sedlar, St. Estèphe

1 cup granulated sugar
1 cup lemon juice
1 cup water
Zest of 3 oranges, 3 grapefruits, and 3 lemons, shredded
1 pound white chocolate
3 cups heavy cream
½ cup pine nuts, chopped or whole
Génoise (recipe page 154), or 1 large loaf sponge or angel food cake
Powdered sugar

Combine the granulated sugar, lemon juice, and water in saucepan. Add the citrus zest; cook until tender. Drain the zest, reserve syrup for another use. Using half of the chocolate, make chocolate curls with a potato peeler. Place the curls on a wax paper-lined tray and freeze to harden. Reserve for garnish.

Melt remaining chocolate in top of a double boiler over barely simmering water. Cool. Whip the cream until stiff. Alternately fold in half the chocolate, half the zest, and half the pine nuts into the cream. Add remaining melted chocolate, half the remaining zest, and half the remaining pine nuts until incorporated into the cream. Reserve the leftover zest and nuts as garnish.

Cut the génoise crosswise into 4 equal rectangular layers, or split a loaf cake into 4 layers. Spread some of the white chocolate frosting on the first layer. Top with another cake layer. Spread with some more frosting. Repeat with next 2 layers. Cover the top and sides with frozen chocolate curls. Delicately place reserved zest and nuts over the chocolate curls. Sprinkle with powdered sugar.

MAKES 1 LARGE CAKE

Génoise

Flour
6 eggs, separated
¾ cup sugar
2 tablespoons Mexican vanilla or 2 teaspoons vanilla extract

Grease, flour, and line the bottom of a 15½ x 10½-inch jelly-roll pan with wax paper. Beat egg yolks with sugar until ribbony. Stir in ¼ cup flour and vanilla. Beat the egg whites until stiff but not dry. Fold into the yolk mixture. Turn into the prepared pan, spreading evenly. Bake at 350 degrees for 20 minutes. Cool.

Note: Store-bought génoise or plain sponge or pound cake may be substituted.

LA MORT AU CHOCOLAT
(Chocolate Death)
Les Anges

Meringue Layer (recipe follows)
Chocolate Génoise (recipe follows)
Chocolate Mousse (recipe follows)
Ganache (recipe page 156)
½ cup toasted chopped almonds
10 to 12 whole filberts
Sliced almonds or filberts

Prepare the meringue layer; set aside. Prepare the chocolate génoise and set aside. (These steps can be prepared well in advance.) Just before assembling, prepare the chocolate mousse and the ganache.

To assemble, spoon half the ganache over the meringue layer in its pan and smooth evenly over the surface. Cut the chocolate génoise into two ¼-inch-thick slices, reserving remaining cake for another use. Place one cake slice over the ganache-meringue layer. Cover with about half the chocolate mousse. Top with the second layer of cake. Spoon remaining mousse over the cake and chill until set, at least 4 to 6 hours.

Just before serving spoon remaining ganache on the cake. Carefully line the sides of the cake with chopped toasted almonds. Decorate top with filbert "roses" by placing the whole filberts evenly around the cake. Place almond slices around each filbert to resemble petals.

MAKES 8 TO 10 SERVINGS

Meringue Layer

⅓ cup egg whites
¾ cup sugar
2 tablespoons unsweetened cocoa

Combine egg whites and sugar in the top of a double boiler. Heat to lukewarm. Remove from heat. Pour into a mixing bowl and beat for about 15 minutes at medium speed, until stiff. Quickly fold in the cocoa to prevent meringue from falling. Grease a 10-inch springform pan, line with parchment paper, and grease again. Pipe the meringue through a pastry bag using a round tube, forming a spiral on the bottom of the springform, starting from the center and working out toward the sides until the bottom is completely covered. Bake at 250 degrees for 2 hours. Cool in pan.

Chocolate Génoise

10 eggs, beaten
¾ cup sugar
1½ cups plus 2 tablespoons flour
2 tablespoons unsweetened cocoa
1 tablespoon butter, melted

Grease a 10 x 3-inch round baking pan, line with parchment paper, and grease again. Combine the beaten eggs and sugar in the top of a double boiler. Heat to lukewarm. Remove from heat. Pour into a mixing bowl and beat on high speed for about 10 minutes or until batter forms a ribbon. Sift the flour and cocoa into batter, and fold to combine. Fold in the butter. Pour the batter into the prepared baking pan and bake at 350 degrees for 35 to 40 minutes or until cake springs back when lightly touched. A wood pick inserted in center should come out clean. Cool thoroughly. Remove from pan.

Chocolate Mousse

1 pound bittersweet chocolate, preferably Belgian
6 egg yolks
8 egg whites
½ cup sugar

Melt the chocolate in the top of a double boiler over simmering water. Remove the pan from the heat and cool. Beat in the egg yolks, one at a time. Beat the egg whites until soft

Gâteau St. Honoré (page 152); White Mousse Cake with Zest of Grapefruit and Pine Nuts (page 153)

peaks form. Gradually beat the sugar into the egg whites; continue beating until stiff peaks form. Lightly fold one-fourth of the beaten whites into the chocolate. Fold in the remaining egg whites, lightly but thoroughly. Chill.

Ganache

6 ounces bittersweet chocolate, preferably Belgian
²/₃ cup heavy cream

Heat the chocolate and cream together in the top of a double boiler over simmering water until the chocolate melts. Blend well.

IL NIDO DOLCE
(The Sweet Nest)
Pasta Etc.

³/₄ cup chocolate angel-hair pasta
³/₄ cup sugar
Crème Anglaise (recipe follows)
Chocolate eggs or egg-shaped truffles, optional

Cook the chocolate angel-hair pasta in 6 quarts boiling water sweetened with sugar until tender, about 7 to 9 minutes. Drain, reserving about 2 tablespoons liquid. Toss with the reserved liquid. Set aside.

Spoon about 2 tablespoons crème anglaise on the bottom of a serving platter. Coil the pasta over the cream layer to resemble a nest. Arrange chocolate eggs in the pasta nest. Chill until ready to serve. Serve with remaining crème Anglaise.

MAKES 4 TO 6 SERVINGS

Crème Anglaise

1 cup heavy cream
6 egg yolks
¼ cup sugar
1 tablespoon grated orange peel
1 teaspoon vanilla extract
1 teaspoon unsalted butter

Scald the cream. Beat the egg yolks with sugar until thick. Gradually pour the scalded cream into the beaten yolk mixture. Turn into a nonaluminum saucepan or skillet. Whisk over medium-high heat until thickened. Remove from heat and stir in the orange peel, vanilla, and butter. Cool, then refrigerate.

MAKES 1½ CUPS

WALNUT BREAD
Rancho Bernardo Inn, San Diego

1 cup butter or margarine, at room temperature
2 cups sugar
4 eggs
4 cups flour
½ teaspoon salt
2 teaspoons baking soda
1½ cups chopped walnuts
2 teaspoons vanilla extract
2 cups sour cream

Cream the butter and sugar until fully blended. Slowly beat in the eggs. Sift the flour, salt, and baking soda, and add to the egg mixture. Blend in the nuts, vanilla, and sour cream. Pour batter into 2 greased and floured 9 x 5-inch loaf pans. Bake at 350 degrees for 45 minutes to 1 hour. Cool in pans for 10 minutes, then invert onto wire rack.

MAKES 2 LOAVES

Note: This bread is excellent when thinly sliced and lightly toasted.

SEED BREAD
Katie Trefethen, Trefethen Vineyards

Water
3 packages dry yeast
1½ tablespoons sugar
3 cups unbleached white flour
1 cup warm milk
2 tablespoons walnut oil
1 tablespoon salt

1 egg
½ cup honey
1½ cups rye flour
1 cup cornmeal
1 cup unprocessed bran
3 cups whole wheat flour
½ cup golden raisins
½ cup chopped walnuts
½ cup sunflower seeds
½ cup poppy seeds
¼ cup caraway seeds
Glaze (recipe follows)

Place ½ cup very warm water in a large, warmed bowl. Swirl water around bowl. Add the yeast and sugar. When mixture is bubbly and light, stir in 1¾ cups warm water, white flour, and warm milk. Set mixture in warm place, covered, until light and doubled in size.

Add the walnut oil, salt, egg, honey, rye flour, cornmeal, bran, whole wheat flour, raisins, walnuts, sunflower seeds, poppy seeds, and caraway seeds. Knead by hand or use dough hook attachment on mixer or processor. Add more white flour as needed. When mixture is no longer sticky, place in a greased bowl, turning to coat. Cover, and allow to rise until doubled.

Punch down. Divide into 3 pieces, so as to have 2 large portions and 1 small portion. Shape into loaves and place the 2 larger loaves in two 9 x 4-inch loaf pans; place the small loaf in a 7½ x 4-inch loaf pan. Let rise to top of pan or slightly over.

Bake at 350 degrees for 50 minutes or until done. Remove from oven and place on racks to cool. Brush with glaze.

MAKES TWO 9 x 4-INCH LOAVES AND ONE 7½ x 4-INCH LOAF

Glaze

1 egg white
1 teaspoon water

Combine the egg white and water. Mix well.

FRESH LEMON ICE

2 teaspoons unflavored gelatin
1¾ cups water
¾ cup sugar
Grated peel of ½ lemon
½ cup lemon juice
2 egg whites

Soften gelatin in ¼ cup water. In a small saucepan combine ½ cup sugar and remaining 1½ cups water. Bring to a boil. Cook 2 minutes. Add gelatin mixture, stirring to dissolve. Add lemon peel and juice. Pour into 8-inch-square pan. Freeze just until mixture becomes slush, about 1½ hours, stirring occasionally.

Beat egg whites until foamy. Gradually add remaining ¼ cup sugar, beating until soft peaks form. Fold beaten egg whites into lemon mixture. Return to freezer. Freeze until firm, stirring occasionally, about another 4 hours.

MAKES 6 SERVINGS

RASPBERRY ICE

2 cups sugar
1 cup water
4 pints raspberries
¼ cup lemon juice
⅓ cup orange juice

Combine the sugar and water in a medium saucepan. Heat and stir until sugar dissolves, then boil for 5 minutes. Cool. Force the raspberries through a food mill or blend in a blender or food processor. Strain to remove seeds if desired. Blend raspberry purée and lemon and orange juices into syrup. Pour into ice cube trays. Wrap trays in foil and freeze. Remove from freezer 20 minutes before serving, and stir a bit to combine the sorbet.

MAKES 8 TO 12 SERVINGS

LEFT: *Il Nido Dolce (page 156)*

BELOW: *Pears and Cream Cheese (page 160)*

RIGHT: *Raspberry Ice ; Fresh Lemon Ice(page 157);*
 Pineapple Sorbet (page 160)

Pineapple Sorbet

1 cup sugar
1¼ cups water
1 very ripe pineapple, cored, peeled, and any "eyes" removed
1 tablespoon lemon juice
1 tablespoon vodka, optional

In a medium saucepan combine sugar and water. Stir well, and bring to a boil. Cover and simmer 5 minutes. Uncover, remove from heat, and set aside.

Cut pineapple into 1-inch chunks. You will need about 2 cups. In a food processor fitted with the steel blade purée 2 cups pineapple chunks until smooth, about 45 seconds. With machine running, pour in half of the hot syrup within 15 seconds. Process 30 seconds; transfer purée to a mixing bowl. Repeat, processing remaining pineapple with remaining sugar syrup. Combine all of the purée. Stir in the lemon juice and vodka.

Transfer pineapple mixture to two shallow pans, dividing evenly. Cover with plastic and freeze until half frozen. Process each batch of partially frozen sorbet mixture for 1 minute, stopping once to scrape down mixture. Return to pans, cover, and freeze until ¾ firm.

Process each batch once again for 1 minute. Return to freezer until ¾ firm, then process another 2 minutes. Pack into an airtight container and freeze until firm enough to scoop or spoon, about 4 to 6 hours.

MAKES 1 QUART

California Fruit Terrine

4 envelopes unflavored gelatin
4 cups white grape juice
3 cups sliced strawberries, approximately
1 to 2 firm-ripe kiwis, peeled and sliced
1 firm-ripe mango, peeled and sliced in thin wedges
1 firm-ripe papaya, peeled and sliced in thin wedges
Fruit Salad Dressing (recipe follows)
Mint sprigs, for garnish

Soften gelatin in 2 cups grape juice. Heat over low heat until dissolved. Stir in remaining 2 cups grape juice. Cool until slightly thickened.

Place a 9-inch loaf pan in a larger pan filled with ice cubes. Pour a small amount of gelatin mixture in bottom of pan to form a thin layer. Arrange one-half of the strawberry slices and all of the kiwi slices in a decorative pattern, *handling kiwis as little as possible*. Allow to set. Carefully, *again without handling too much*, arrange mango slices over surface to form another layer. Spoon over more gelatin mixture to cover fruit. Again, allow to set.

Top with layer of remaining sliced strawberries. Spoon over more gelatin mixture to cover berries. Allow to set. Top with papaya slices. Pour over remaining gelatin mixture. Chill until completely set.

Unmold onto serving platter and cut into slices about ¾-inch thick. Serve each slice with a dollop of fruit salad dressing. Garnish with mint sprigs and more fresh fruit, if desired.

MAKES ABOUT 8 SERVINGS

Note: Be careful to handle papaya, mangos, and kiwi slices as little as possible. Do not try to mix into gelatin mixture or gelatin will not set. Any other sliced or cut fruit may be substituted.

Fruit Salad Dressing

¼ cup honey
½ cup mayonnaise
½ cup heavy cream, whipped
1 to 2 tablespoons raspberry or other fruit purée

Blend honey, mayonnaise, and whipped cream. Add fruit purée.

MAKES 1½ CUPS

Pears and Cream Cheese

8 ounces cream cheese, softened
1 to 2 tablespoons black raspberry liqueur
4 large pears
Lemon juice
Chopped pistachio nuts
Mint leaves, for garnish

Stir together the cream cheese and raspberry liqueur. Slice the pears in half lengthwise. Hollow out the centers with a teaspoon or melon baller. Dip the pears in lemon juice to prevent browning. Spoon cream cheese into the pear centers and sprinkle with pistachio nuts. Garnish with mint leaves.

MAKES 8 SERVINGS

CRANBERRY-ORANGE TART

1 cup slivered almonds
1/2 cup butter, cut up
Brown sugar
1 1/2 cups flour
1 egg
1/4 cup orange juice
1 envelope unflavored gelatin
1 cup orange marmalade
4 1/2 cups fresh or frozen cranberries

In a food processor chop the almonds until ground. Add the butter, 3 tablespoons brown sugar, 1 cup of the flour, and the egg. Cover, and process till mixture forms a ball. Add remaining flour. Cover and process again until mixture forms ball. Press the dough into a 9-inch springform pan, forming a 2-inch-high crust on all sides. Chill the crust for 20 minutes. Bake at 350 degrees for 20 to 25 minutes, or until edges are golden. Cool.

In a saucepan stir together the orange juice and gelatin until gelatin dissolves. Stir in 2/3 cup marmalade and 1/2 to 3/4 cup brown sugar. Bring mixture to a boil. Stir in the cranberries. Reduce heat to a simmer; cover and simmer 10 minutes. Remove from heat and skim off foam. Pour mixture into the cooled crust. Chill tart for several hours or overnight.

To serve, remove sides of springform pan and place the tart on serving platter. Melt remaining marmalade and brush over the tart.

MAKES ONE 9-INCH TART

ZUCCHINI BREAD

2 cups flour
1/4 teaspoon baking powder
2 teaspoons baking soda
1 tablespoon ground cinnamon
1/2 teaspoon ground cloves
1/2 teaspoon ground nutmeg
1 teaspoon salt
3 eggs
1 cup oil
1/2 cup brown sugar, packed
1 cup granulated sugar
2 teaspoons vanilla extract
3 cups shredded zucchini
1 cup chopped walnuts
1 cup raisins

Sift the flour, baking powder, soda, cinnamon, cloves, nutmeg, and salt. Beat the eggs in a large mixing bowl very briefly. Turn speed to low and gradually add oil, both sugars, and vanilla. Mix about 2 minutes, or until thoroughly combined. Add sifted ingredients, mixing until blended. Fold in zucchini, nuts, and raisins.

Divide batter into 2 well-greased 8 x 4-inch loaf pans and bake at 350 degrees for 1 hour and 15 minutes, or until loaves test done. Remove to wire rack and cool 10 minutes. Remove from pans and cool completely.

MAKES 2 LOAVES

Note: If desired add 1 (8 3/4-ounce) can crushed pineapple, drained, to batter along with the zucchini.

VANILLA SOUFFLÉ

Butter
Sugar
1/4 cup flour
1 1/4 cups milk
4 eggs, separated
1 teaspoon vanilla extract
1/4 teaspoon cream of tartar
Powdered sugar

Butter the bottom of a 1 1/2-quart soufflé dish well. Sprinkle 1 to 2 tablespoons sugar evenly over it. Set aside. In a saucepan whisk together the flour, 2 tablespoons sugar, and 1/3 cup milk. Place over medium heat and whisk in remaining milk. Cook, stirring, until mixture thickens. Remove from heat. Lightly beat the egg yolks and stir in with 2 tablespoons butter and vanilla. Set aside.

Beat the egg whites with the cream of tartar until soft peaks form. Sprinkle 1 tablespoon sugar over whites and continue beating until stiff peaks form. Spoon 1/3 of the egg whites into the cream sauce and whisk until just blended. Pour blended mixture over remaining egg whites and gently fold mixtures together. Spoon batter into the prepared soufflé dish and bake at 325 degrees for 50 to 55 minutes or until soufflé is high and a deep golden brown. Remove from oven, quickly sprinkle with powdered sugar, and serve at once.

MAKES 6 SERVINGS

Vanilla Soufflé (page 161)

CREDITS

Larry Armstrong, 7 (bottom right), 23, 139 (top); Brent Bear, 34, 66 (bottom), 67, 74, 99, 114, 126 (bottom and center); Myron Beck, 7 (bottom left), 130; Larry Bessel, 10, 30 (bottom), 82 (top), 83, 158 (top), 166 (all); Henry Bjoin, 42, 135 (top), 159; Mark Boster, 66 (top), 122; Richard Clark, 22 (both), 127 (top); Larry Davis, 6 (top left), 19, 127 (bottom); Patrick Downs, 14, 119; Ian Dryden, 39 (both), 54 (bottom), 75; Michael Edwards, 7 (top right; bottom center), 26 (all), 30 (top), 98 (bottom left), 146 (top); Scott Flynn, 6 (bottom left), 98 (bottom right); Jerry Fruchtman, 135 (bottom), 139 (bottom); George De Gennaro, 86, 143, 150, 155, 162; Penni Gladstone, 6 (top right), 70 (top), 123; Ken Hively, 90, 102 (bottom); Peter Hogg, 47, 50 (top), 51, 70 (bottom), 79, 110, 111, 142; Randy Leffingwell, 31, 38, 50 (bottom), 54 (top), 94, 146 (bottom left and right), 151 (both), 158 (bottom); Rick Mayer, 55, 90 (top), 147; Randy McBride, 27, 58, 62; Jim McHugh, 2, 126 (top); Richard Ruthsatz, 7 (top left), 102 (top), 103, 107, 138 (both); Dick Sharpe, 91; Bob Stein, 98 (top); Richard Sullivan, 82 (bottom), 167; Fritz Taggart, 6 (bottom right).

STYLISTS

Minnie Bernardino; Marlene Brown; Donna Deane; Marya Dosti; Rose Dosti; Olivia Erschen; Janet Miller; Maggi Miller; Carol Peterson; Lorraine Triolo; Robin Tucker.

ACKNOWLEDGMENTS

Newspaper cookbooks involve compiling recipes from many sources, and in this case contributors include restaurant chefs here in Los Angeles and north to San Francisco, culinary organizations, and amateur home cooks. Just as important are the many *Los Angeles Times* editors, writers, copy editors, food stylists, photographers, and typists in shaping and contributing to this book.

A special mention of appreciation goes to: Betsy Balsley, the food editor of the *Los Angeles Times,* for her enthusiastic support; Robin Tucker, creative director of food for the *Los Angeles Times Magazine,* for her artistic contributions; Alfred Beck, art director of the *Times Magazine;* Terrence E. Redknapp, associate design director of the *Times;* Minnie Bernardino, Donna Deane, Deborah Brown, and their predecessors in the kitchen staff for recipe testing—all the recipes in the book have, in one way or another, passed through their skillful hands.

Thanks also to staffers Daniel Puzo, Karen Gillingham, Joan Drake, Nancy Farr, Marge Powers, and Melanie Clarkson for their contributions.

I am grateful as well to Angela Rinaldi, of the *Times* Syndicate, whose original ideas and creative direction were invaluable.

To Darlene Geis and, particularly, Ruth Peltason—the Abrams editors who questioned, questioned, and questioned—and to the rest of the Abrams staff who produced this book, thank you all.

ROSE DOSTI

INDEX

Abalone salad, 71
Adriano's Ristorante, 88
ahi carpaccio, 18
Albrecht, Werner, 65, 96, 133
Allen, Joe, 104
almond(s)
   and chicken with pasta, 92–3
   tart, lemon curd, 148
   tile, Udo's, 152
Alrivy, Claude, 18
ancho chili butter with chicken paillard, 117
Angeli, 134
Antoine, Hotel Meridien, 101
appetizers. *see* starters
apricots, in holiday charlotte, 152
arista (pork roast), 134
arroz con pollo á la Cubana, 129
artichoke(s)
   bottoms in summer vegetable plate, 61
   tiny, in vegetables à la Grecque, 52
   vinaigrette, 45
arugula, in quails with summer vegetables, 121
Ash, John, 9, 134
asparagus
   asperges aux arrowroot vinaigrette de prune
     (*asparagus in a blanket with
     plum vinaigrette*), 68
   cold, poached, with flavored mayonnaise, 45
   with duck pâté, 20
   sauté, Chinese, 53
Athenian pizza, 93
Au Relais, 136
avocado(s)
   chef salad, 77
   in salade mikado, 65
   in snapper salad, 71–2
   in warm scallop salad with roasted red
     peppers, 69

Baglioni, Emilio, 8
balsamic
   dressing, 46
   vinegar dressing, 68
barbecue, Korean
   beef, 141
   chicken, 141
   pork, 141
Bardot, Camille, 8
basil
   in pasta pesto, 81
   red pepper sauce, 13
   in roasted sea bass with crust of herbs, 101
bean(s)
   brown, and radicchio salad, 64
   green, nest with scallop eggs, 68–9
   green, in picnic vegetable salad, 64
   see also kidney beans
béchamel sauce, 87
beef
   ground, in meatloaf, 137
   ground, in ragout for leopard's dish, 87
   in Korean barbecue, 141
   roast, in avocado chef salad, 77
   sirloin, in Chinese fire pot, 41, 43
   steak in kushikatsu, 17
beer batter, 49
Bellisario, Giuseppe, 133
beluga butter with three-color tamales, 25
Beringer Vineyards, 12, 28, 48, 60, 69, 131, 132
Bernard's, 8, 46, 52
Bertranou, Jean, 8
Beverly Pavilion Hotel, 48, 61, 105
Bistro, The, 8
Bistro Garden, 120
Black, Cindy, 120
blackberry/ies
   ice cream, Pauline's, 145

   in neon tumbleweed with cactus cookies, 149
   in summer fruit with fromage blanc, 145
Blanchet, Michel, 8, 97
blue corn tortillas with smoked salmon and
     American caviar, 28
Blue Fox, 8
Boh!, 81
Border Grill, 9, 21
boucheron cheese, in calzone, 84–5
bouillabaisse, California, 112
bread
   seed, 156–7
   walnut, 156
   zucchini, 161
broccoli torte, 45–6
brochettes of lamb, 132
Brody, Bob, 80, 81, 104
Brown Derby, The, 8
Bruggemans, Paul, 8
bul-kogi (*Korean barbecue*), 141
butter
   ancho chili, 117
   beluga, 25
   wash, 61

Cabernet dressing, 72
cake
   gâteau St. Honoré, 152
   génoise, 154
     chocolate, 154
   Montmartre, 153
   la mort au chocolat (*chocolate death*), 154
   white mousse with zest of grapefruit and pine
     nuts, 153
California
   bouillabaisse, 112

corn salad, composed, 77
    fruit terrine, 160
calzone, 84–5
Camelions, 9, 13, 46
cannelloni, spinach, 89
cantaloupes, in Hawaiian chicken salad, 78
caramel sauce, 149
carp, in Hunan-style steamed fish, 109
Carpenter, Hugh, 76
carrot(s)
    baby, in summer vegetable plate, 61
    mushroom ragout, 46
    in vegetable chili, 53
catfish fillets, baked, with horseradish sauce,
    109
cauliflower, in vegetables à la Grecque, 52
caviar
    American, with smoked salmon and blue
      corn tortillas, 28
    American, in snapper salad, 71–2
    beluga butter, 25
celery
    and chicken with kushikatsu, 17
    in vegetable chili, 53
Celestino Ristorante, 85
Chan Dara Siamese Kitchen, 87
chanterelle(s)
    with duck pâté, 20
    in paupiette de dorade rouge, 100
    with pigeon and baby California
      vegetables, 124–5
    sauce, 108
    in snapper salad, 71–2
charlotte, holiday, 152
Chasen's, 8
Chaya Brasserie, 9
cheddar cheese, in cheese sauce, 56
cheese
    appetizer and jumbo shells, 32
    mixed, filling for pizza rustica, 88
    sauce, 56
    see also under boucheron, cheddar, chèvre,
      cream, feta, fromage blanc, goat,
      mozzarella, Parmesan, pecorino, pecorino
      romano, romano, ricotta, Sonoma, tuma
Chenel, Laura, 12, 116, 144
chèvre
    baked with garden salad, 61
    crème de, 24
    in plumped poussin, 117
    in summer fruit with fromage blanc, 145
Chez Panisse, 9, 12, 61, 84
chicken
    and almonds with pasta, 92–3

arroz con pollo á la Cubana, 128
barbecue, Korean, 141
breasts in Chinese fire pot, 41
breasts in satay, 17
breasts in spinach cannelloni, 89
broth, far east, 41
burger, 120
with celery in kushikatsu, 17
fun see, 117, 120
galantine with corn and red pepper, 21
livers in kushikatsu, 17
livers in pâté Diana, 32–3
orange honeyed, 128
paillard with ancho chili butter, 117
plumped poussin, 117
salad, Hawaiian, 78
salad, mai fun, 78
salad, Spanish, 78
smoked in fiddlehead fern salad, 73
in sopa de tortilla, 37, 40
stock dressing, 73
terrine, southwestern, 33–4
and zucchini stir-fried, 128
chile(s)
    green, mayonnaise, 97
    green, stuffed with mushroom duxelles, 24
    orange mayonnaise, 21
    rellenos, 21, 24
chili
    ancho, butter with chicken paillard, 117
    vegetable, 53
Chinese
    asparagus sauté, 53
    fire pot, 41, 43
Chinois on Main, 8, 71
chocolate
    dark, in holiday charlotte, 152
    filling for gâteau St. Honoré, 152
    ganache, 156
    génoise, 154
    il nido dolce (*the sweet nest*), 156
    la mort au chocolat (*chocolate death*), 154
    mousse, 154, 156
Chung, Henry, 48
cider, hard, with pan-roasted quails, 120–21
cilantro sauce, 34
Cirino, Bruno, 101
citrus-ginger sauce, 13
City restaurant, 9, 152
clams
    in California bouillabaisse, 112
    with corn mousse, 108
    in kushikatsu, 17
    in Trumps seafood salad for one, 72

Club Culinaire Français de Californie, 52, 132
cod, in Sarasota fish soup, 41
Colette, 9, 48, 61, 105
confetti penne, 92
cookies
    cactus, with neon tumbleweed, 149
    Udo's almond tile, 152
corn
    mousse with clams (*mousse de maïs aux
      palourdes*), 108
    pudding, 56
    and red pepper with galantine, 21
    salad, composed California, 77
    salmon, and jalapeños terrine, 97
cornish game hens, grilled, 125
crab
    cracked, North Beach, 113
    legs in California bouillabaisse, 112
    legs or slices in kushikatsu, 17
cranberry-orange tart, 161
cream
    hazelnut, 148
    pastry, 148
cream cheese and pears, 160
cream sauce for black and white tortelli, 32
crème Anglaise, 156
cucumber
    in picnic vegetable salad, 76–7
    soup, 36

Danko, Gary, 12, 28, 48, 69, 131, 132, 148
David, Narsai, 9
demi-glace, quick, for sweetbreads, 140
Dover sole Olympiad, paupiette de, 97, 100
Drago, Celestino, 85
dressing
    balsamic, 46
    balsamic vinegar, 68
    cabernet, 72
    chicken stock, 73
    fruit salad, 160
    hoisin, 78
    lemon juice and olive oil, 89
    vinaigrette, 92
    wild watercress, 106
    see also under vinaigrette
dried tomatoes, 57
duck
    pâté, 20
    salad, gyoza, 73, 76
duckling with mole sauce, 128

Eel, freshwater, in Tommy's roll, 13
eggs
    in jelly, 89
    with salmon and sorrel sauce, 88–9
    sweet, 16
eggplant(s)
    baby, in ragout of vegetables, 52–3
    grilled salad, 64
    in grilled vegetables, 117
    Japanese, grilled, 46
    Japanese, in vegetables à la Grecque, 52
    sandwiches, 28
    squid and shrimp sauté, 104–05
    stacks, 56
Emilio's, 8
enoki mushrooms
    in grilled tuna salad, 100
    in salade mikado, 65
    in tagliarini verde al capra, 84
Ernie's, 8

Farfalle, Rex's, 81
Feniger, Susan, 9, 21, 144, 152
fennel in grilled vegetables, 117
Ferry, Gerard and Virginie, 8
feta, in grilled prawn salad, 71
fettuccine
    in pasta salad with three bell peppers, 84
    in Szechuan noodle salad in peanut sauce, 76
    in tagliarini verde al capra, 84
fiddlehead fern and smoked chicken salad, 73
fillet mosaic with red pepper sauce, 112
filo cheese cups, savory, 28–9
First Street Bar and Grill, The, 105
fish
    fillets in Chinese fire pot, 41
    fillets in San Pedro cioppino, 40
    steamed Hunan-style, 109
    see also under carp, catfish, cod, Dover sole,
        eel, haddock, halibut, red snapper,
        salmon, sea bass, snapper, sole, squid,
        tuna
Five-Star Catering Co. Inc., 65, 96, 133
Fournou's Oven, 8
Frank, Ken, 8, 9, 49, 84, 100
fromage blanc
    filling for savory filo cheese cups, 29
    with peaches in summer fruit, 145
fruit
    salad dressing, 160

    summer, with fromage blanc, 145
    tarts, 145, 148
    terrine, California, 160
    see also under individual names
Fukui, Susumu, 9, 68, 100
fun see chicken, 117, 120

Galantine with corn and red pepper, 21
game hens, grilled, 125
ganache, 156
garlic and green onions stir-fried with oysters,
    106
gâteau St. Honoré, 152
gazpacho, 37
    yogurt, 43
Gelson's Market, 53
génoise, 154
    chocolate, 154
Gernreich, Rudy, 35, 36
Gibert, Roland, 46, 52
Gilmore, Elka, 9, 13, 46
Giuseppe!, 133
glaze for bread, 157
goat cheese baked with garden salad, 61
grapefruit zest and pine nuts with white mousse
    cake, 153
gravy for meatloaf, 137
green peppercorn sauce
    with shrimp, 104
    with veal fillet, 133
green sauce on grilled tuna salad, 101
gremolata for osso buco, 134
Grill, The, 136
gyoza duck salad, 73, 76

Haddock in Sarasota fish soup, 41
halibut
    in California bouillabaisse, 112
    in Sarasota fish soup, 41
ham
    in avocado chef salad, 77
    in ris de veau sous cloche Virginienne, 140
Hawaiian chicken salad, 78
hazelnut cream, 148
Healy, Patrick, 9, 48, 61, 105
herbs, crust of, with roasted sea bass, 101, 104

hoisin dressing, 78
holiday charlotte, 142
honeydew melons, in Hawaiian chicken salad,
    78
honeyed orange chicken, 128
horseradish sauce with baked catfish fillets, 109
Hotel Bel-Air, 9, 101, 106
Hotel Meridien, 101
Huegli, Ueli, 88
Hunan Restaurant, The, 48
Hunan-style steamed fish (*to sze tsen yui*), 109
hunter's toast (*crostini di cacciagione*), 20

Ice
    lemon, 157
    raspberry, 157
ice cream
    Pauline's blackberry, 145
    Santa Rosa plum, 145
il nido dolce (*the sweet nest*), 156
Inner Gourmet, 28, 37, 45, 65, 69
Italian salad, 68

Jacoupy, Bernard, 8
jalapeño(s)
    corn and salmon terrine, 97
    jelly, 57
Jamon, Patrick, 154
jicama, in fried lumpia, 140
Jimmy's, 36
John Ash & Co., 9, 134

Kiwi(s)
    in holiday charlotte, 152
    in neon tumbleweed with cactus cookies, 149
Kleiman, Evan, 134
Korean barbecue, bul-kogi, 141
Kranwinkle, Susan, 28, 37, 45, 65, 69
kung tom yam (Thai prawn soup), 37, 40
kushikatsu, 16–17

Lamb
brochettes, 132
Narsai's pomegranate, 132
rack of, artillery, 143
shanks, 132
la mort au chocolat (*chocolate death*), 154
La Petite Chaya, 9, 68, 100
La Place, Viana, 134
La Scala, 8, 104
La Toque, 49, 84, 100
Le Chardonnay, 18
Le Petit Four, 152
Le St. Germain, 8, 64
leeks au gratin, 56
lemon
curd, almond tart, 148
ice, fresh, 157
juice and olive oil dressing, 89
leopard's dish, the (*timballo di pasta alla Siciliana*), 85, 87
L'Ermitage, 8, 97
Les Anges, 154
lettuce, salmon fillets grilled in, 108–09
lime butter with scallops, 105
linguine, in pasta pesto, 81
lobster
tails in California bouillabaisse, 112
with wild watercress dressing, 106
L'Orangerie, 8, 124
Louis M. Martini Winery, 89
lumpia, fried, 140

Macaroni, corkscrew, with spinach pesto, 81
Madame Wu's Garden, 8, 117
madeira sauce, 121
mai fun chicken salad, 78
Ma Maison, 8, 64
Mandarin, The, 124
Marchesan, Claudio, 28, 68
marinara sauce, 89
marmalade, onion, toast, 18
Martini, Liz, 89
Maui onion rings, 48
Max au Triangle, 9, 49, 108
Maximin, Jacques, 9
mayonnaise
green chile, 97
orange-chile, 21
McCarty, Michael, 8, 9

meat. *see under* beef, ham, lamb, pork, sweetbreads, veal
meatloaf 72 Market Street, 137
meringue layer, 154
Michael's, 8, 12, 18, 48, 71, 121
mignonette sauce, 13
Milliken, Mary Sue, 9, 21, 144, 152
mirin sauce, for pork tenderloin, 134
miso dip, 16
mole sauce with duckling, 128
Mon Kee Restaurant, 106
Montmartre, 153
mousse
chocolate, 154, 156
salmon, 25
salmon with Dover sole, 97
scallop, 25
spinach, 25
mozzarella
in calzone, 84–5
in the leopard's dish, 85
mushroom(s)
carrot ragout, 46
duxelles in stuffed green chiles, 24
in grilled vegetables, 117
minced in fried lumpia, 140
wild, sauce with roast veal loin and shallots, 132–3
see also under chanterelle, enoki, shiitake
mussels
in California bouillabaisse, 112
in Trumps seafood salad for one, 72
Musso & Frank Grill, 8, 132
mustard sauce, 120

Narsai's, 9, 45
Narsai's pomegranate lamb, 132
neon tumbleweed with cactus cookies, 149
noodle(s)
spiral, in walnut pasta salad, 92
Szechuan, salad in peanut sauce, 76

Oba leaves in grilled tuna salad, 100
olive oil and lemon juice dressing, 89

onion(s)
cakes, 48
green, and garlic stir-fried with oysters, 106
green, in snapper salad, 71–2
marmalade toast, 18
rings, Maui, 46
soup, 36–7
orange
chile mayonnaise, 21
cranberry tart, 161
honeyed chicken, 128
oriental treasure soup, 41
Orlando-Orsini Ristorante, 20
osso buco, 133–4
oyster(s)
in California bouillabaisse, 112
sauce, 124
stir-fried with garlic and green onions, 106
with three sauces, 13
in Trumps seafood salad for one, 72

Pacific Dining Car, 136
pad Thai, 87
panada, 21
pancakes, potato, 121
papaya(s)
in holiday charlotte, 152
in neon tumbleweed with cactus cookies, 149
with shrimp piquant, 69
Parmesan
in pasta pesto, 81
in vitello marinato Parmigiano e olio di tartufo, 18
pasta
with chicken and almonds, 92–3
corkscrew macaroni with spinach pesto, 81
the leopard's dish (*timballo di pasta alla Siciliana*), 85, 87
nibbles, crisp-fried, 28
pad Thai, 87
penne, confetti, 92
pesto, 81
Rex's farfalle, 81
salad
with three bell peppers, 84
wagon wheel, 92
walnut, 92
spinach cannelloni, 89
Szechuan noodle salad in peanut sauce, 76

with Szechuan spiced shrimp, 81, 84
    tagliarini verde al capra, 84
    tortelli, black and white-on-a-stick, 29–30,
        32
Pasta Etc., 84, 144, 156
pastry cream, 148
pâté Diana, 32–3
pâté, duck, 20
patty pan squash
    baby, in quails with summer vegetables, 121
    in ragout of baby vegetables, 52–3
    in snapper salad, 71–2
Pauline's blackberry ice cream, 145
paupiette de
    dorade rouge, 100
    Dover sole Olympiad, 97, 100
peaches
    in holiday charlotte, 152
    in summer fruit with fromage blanc, 145
peanut butter sauce, 17
peanut sauce, 76
pears
    and cream cheese, 160
    in holiday charlotte, 152
peas. see under snow peas, sugar snap peas
pecan tarts, 148–9
pecorino cheese
    in mixed cheese filling for pizza rustica, 88
pecorino romano cheese
    in pasta pesto, 81
penne
    confetti, 92
    in the leopard's dish, 85, 87
pepper(s), bell
    stuffed, in kushikatsu, 17
    three, with pasta salad, 84
pepper(s), jalapeño. see under jalapeño(s)
pepper(s), red
    basil sauce, 13
    with corn and galantine, 21
    in grilled vegetables, 117
    roasted with warm scallop salad, 69
    sauce, 112
    soup, 36
    and tomato sauce, 30
Peppone's pork scaloppine, 136
pesto
    pasta, 81
    spinach, 81
picnic vegetable salad, 76–7
pie pastry for leopard's dish, 87
pigeon with chanterelles and baby California
        vegetables, 124–5
pimiento-wrapped Italian sausage, 137

pineapple(s)
    in neon tumbleweed with cactus cookies, 149
    sorbet, 160
pine nuts
    in pasta pesto, 81
    and zest of grapefruit with white mousse
        cake, 153
Piret's, 120
pizza
    Athenian, 93
    calzone, 84–5
    dough, 85
    rustica, 88
pork
    arista, 134
    chop, smoked in arroz con pollo á la Cubana,
        29
    crown of, with saffron rice stuffing, 141, 143
    Dijonnaise, 136
    ground, in fried lumpia, 140
    ground, in meatloaf 72 Market Street, 137
    Korean barbecue, 141
    lean, in pad Thai, 87
    scaloppine, Peppone's, 136
    tenderloin of, Kobe-style, 134
potato/es
    with kushikatsu, 17
    new, in paupiette de dorade rouge, 100
    pancakes, 121
    in picnic vegetable salad, 76–7
    salt-roasted, 48
poussin, plumped, 117
prawn salad, grilled, 71
prawns, in scampi mare nostrum, 104
Prego, 28, 68
Primi, 29
prosciutto
    in calzone, 84–5
    in the leopard's dish, 85, 87
    in mixed cheese filling, 88
Puck, Wolfgang, 8, 9, 64, 71, 80, 88

Quails
    pan-roasted, with hard cider, 120–21
    with summer vegetables, 121
Quattrucci, Mario, 20
Quenioux, Laurent, 9, 20, 96

Rack of lamb, artillery, 143
radicchio
    and bean salad, 64
    salad grilled, 64
ragout
    of baby vegetables, 52–3
    carrot-mushroom, 41
    for leopard's dish, 87
Rahn, Peggy, 28, 37, 45, 65, 69
Rancho Bernardo Inn, 156
raspberry/ies
    in gyoza duck salad, 73
    ice, 96
    in neon tumbleweed with cactus cookies, 149
    vinaigrette, 96
ratatouille, shrimp, stuffing for small
        vegetables, 49, 52
red pepper. see pepper(s), red
red sauce on grilled tuna salad, 101
red snapper
    in California bouillabaisse, 112
    Chinois, 113
    fillets in paupiette de dorade rouge, 100
    in snapper salad, 71–2
red wine sauce with smoke-roasted squab, 123
Rex's farfalle, 81
Rex Il Ristorante, 8, 18, 64, 81
rice
    risotto Milanese, 88
    saffron, 93
    saffron stuffing for crown of pork, 143
    sweet, 16
Richard, Michel, 144, 145, 153
ricotta cheese, in mixed cheese filling for pizza
        rustica, 88
ris de veau sous cloche Virginienne, 140
risotto Milanese, 88
Roberts, Michael, 8, 9, 72, 73, 125
romano cheese
    in mixed cheese filling for pizza rustica, 88

Saffron
    rice, 93
    rice stuffing for crown of pork, 141, 143
    sauce for Dover sole, 97, 100
    sauce with stuffed scallop surprise, 105–06
St. Estéphe, 24, 25, 28, 95, 97, 144, 149, 153

salads
  abalone, 71
  asperges aux arrowroot vinaigrette de prune
    (*asparagus in a blanket with plum
    vinaigrette*), 68
  avocado chef, 77
  baked goat cheese with garden salad, 61
  bean and radicchio, 64
  composed California corn, 77
  fiddlehead fern and smoked chicken, 73
  green bean nest with scallop eggs, 68–9
  grilled eggplant, 64
  grilled prawn, 71
  grilled radicchio, 64
  grilled tuna, 100
  gyoza duck, 73, 76
  Hawaiian chicken, 78
  Italian, 68
  mai fun chicken, 78
  papaya with shrimp piquant, 69
  picnic vegetable, 76–7
  portable picnic spinach, 65
  salade mikado with tarragon vinaigrette, 65
  snapper, 71–2
  Spanish chicken, 78
  summer vegetable plate, 61
  Szechuan noodle in peanut sauce, 76
  Trumps seafood salad for one, 72
  wagon wheel pasta, 92
  walnut pasta, 92
  warm scallop with roasted red peppers, 69
  warm vegetable with truffles, 64–5
salami, Italian, in mixed cheese filling, 88
Salmagundi, 37
salmon
  corn, and jalapeños terrine, 97
  fillet in Trumps seafood salad for one, 72
  fillets grilled in lettuce, 108–09
  fillets in fillet mosaic with red pepper sauce,
    112
  fillets in tournedos de saumon, 96
  mousse, 25
  mousse with Dover sole, 97
  poached, chilled, 108
  in raspberry vinaigrette, 96
  and sorrel sauce with eggs, 88–9
salmon, smoked
  with blue corn tortillas and American caviar,
    28
  in Tommy's roll, 13
salsa
  green, 24
  green chile, 73
  party, 32

  red, 24, 72
sandwich/es
  eggplant, 28
  Trumps Cuban, 124
sandwich filling
  poultry or meat, 125
  seafood salad, 125
San Pedro cioppino, 40
Santa Rosa plum ice cream, 145
Sarasota fish soup, 41
satay, 17
sauce
  basil-red pepper, 13
  béchamel, 87
  caramel, 149
  chanterelle, 108
  cheese, 56
  cilantro, 34
  citrus-ginger, 13
  cream, for tortelli, 32
  green, 101
  madeira, 121
  marinara, 89
  mignonette, 13
  mirin, for pork tenderloin, 134
  mustard, 120
  oyster, 124
  peanut, 76
  peanut butter, 17
  red, 101
  saffron, 100, 106
  salsa
    green, 24
    green chile, 73
    party, 32
    red, 24, 72
  sweet-sour, 140
  tomato
    raw, 52
    raw yellow, 52
    red pepper, 30
  tonkatsu, 16
  truffle, 18
  wild watercress, 107
sausage, Italian
  in mixed cheese filling for pizza, 88
  pimiento-wrapped, 137
scallop(s)
  eggs in green bean nest, 68–9
  in kushikatsu, 17
  with lime butter, 105
  mousse, 25
  salad, warm, with roasted red peppers, 69
  surprise, stuffed, with saffron sauce, 105–06

  in Trumps seafood salad for one, 72
  in Venice Beach seafood soup, 40–41
scampi mare nostrum, 104
Scandia, 8, 37
Schwartz, Leonard, 137
sea bass
  in California bouillabaisse, 112
  roasted with crust of herbs, 101, 104
seafood
  filling for tortelli, 30
  salad filling, 125
  salad for one, Trumps, 72
  soup, Venice Beach, 40–41
  see also under fish and shellfish
seaweed
  in kushikatsu, 17
  squares in Tommy's roll, 13
Sedlar, John, 9, 24, 25, 28, 95, 97, 144, 149, 153
seed bread, 156–7
Selvaggio, Piero, 8, 29
Seventh Street Bistro, 9, 20, 96
72 Market Street, 137
shallots with roast veal loin and wild mushroom
    sauce, 132–3
shellfish. *see under* abalone, clams, crabs,
    lobster, mussels, prawn, scallops, scampi,
    shrimp
shells, jumbo, and cheese appetizers, 32
Sheraton Harbor Island West, 80, 81, 104
shiitake mushrooms
  in abalone salad, 71
  in paupiette de dorade rouge, 100
  in salade mikado, 65
  sauté, 53
short ribs, braised, 134
shrimp
  bisque, 37
  in California bouillabaisse, 112
  in Chinese fire pot, 41, 43
  chopped, in fried lumpia, 140
  with green peppercorn sauce, 104
  jumbo, in Trumps seafood salad for one, 72
  in kung tom yam, 40
  in kushikatsu, 17
  in pad Thai, 87
  piquant, with papaya, 69
  ratatouille, 49, 52
  in San Pedro cioppino, 40
  squid, and eggplant sauté, 104–05
  Szechuan spiced, with pasta, 81, 84
  in Venice Beach seafood soup, 40–41
Siamese Princess Restaurant, 17
Siegfried, Linda, 116, 144
snapper salad, 71–2

snow peas
  in abalone salad, 71
  in summer vegetable plate, 61
Sodsook, Victor, 17
sole fillets, in fillet mosaic with red-pepper
    sauce, 112
Sonoma goat cheese, in calzone, 84–5
sopa de tortilla, 37, 40
sorbet, pineapple, 160
sorrel and salmon sauce with eggs, 88–9
Sorrento Italian Market, 88
soufflé, vanilla, 161
soup
  Chinese fire pot, 41, 43
  cucumber, 36
  gazpacho, 37
    yogurt, cold, 43
  onion, 36–7
  oriental treasure, 41
  red pepper, 36
  San Pedro cioppino, 40
  shrimp bisque, 37
  sopa de tortilla, 37, 40
  Thai prawn, 40
  Venice Beach seafood, 40–41
sour cream-yogurt filling, 153
Spago, 8, 64, 148
Spanish chicken salad, 78
spinach
  cannelloni, 89
  mousse, 25
  pesto, 81
  salad, portable picnic, 65
  in stuffed scallop surprise with saffron sauce,
    105–06
Splichal, Joachim, 9, 49, 108
squab
  minced (Chinese tacos), 124
  smoke-roasted, with red wine sauce, 123
squash
  baby corn, in small stuffed vegetables, 49, 52
  baby yellow, in ragout of vegetables, 52–3
  summer, in grilled vegetables, 117
  see also under patty pan and zucchini
squid
  shrimp, and eggplant sauté, 104–05
  in Trumps seafood salad for one, 72
Stars, 9, 117, 123
starters
  ahi carpaccio, 18
  black and white tortelli-on-a-stick, 29–30, 32
  blue corn tortillas with smoked salmon and
    American caviar, 28

chiles rellenos, 21
crisp-fried pasta nibbles, 28
duck pâté, 20
  with chanterelles or asparagus, 20
eggplant sandwiches, 28
galantine with corn and red pepper, 21
green chiles stuffed with mushroom
    duxelles, 24
hunter's toast (crostini di cacciagione), 20
jumbo shells and cheese appetizers, 32
kushikatsu, 16
onion marmalade toast, 18
oysters with three sauces, 13
party salsa, 32–3
pâté Diana, 32–3
satay, 17
savory filo cheese cups, 28
southwestern chicken terrine, 33
three-color tamales with beluga butter, 25
Tommy's roll, 13
vitello marinato Parmigiano e olio di tartufo,
    18
steak, in kushikatsu, 17
sugar snap pea stuffing for vine-ripened
    tomatoes, 48
summer
  fruit with fromage blanc, 145
  squash in grilled vegetables, 117
  vegetable plate, 61
sweet
  eggs, 16
  rice, 16
sweetbreads, in ris de veau sous cloche
    Virginienne, 140
sweet-sour sauce for fried lumpia, 140
Szechuan
  noodle salad in peanut sauce, 76
  spiced shrimp with pasta, 81, 84

Tagliarini verde al capra, 84
tamales, three-color, with beluga butter, 24
tamarind juice, in pad Thai, 87
Tang, Tommy, 13
tangerine-butter sauce with tuna, 101
tarragon vinaigrette, 65
tart(s)
  almond, lemon curd, 148
  cranberry-orange, 161
  fruit, 145, 148

pecan, 148–9
shells, 148
tenderloin of pork Kobe-style, 134
Terrail, Patrick, 8, 64
terrine
  California fruit, 156
  of salmon, corn, and jalapeños, 97
  southwestern chicken, 33
Thai prawn soup, 40
385 North, 9, 21, 71, 73
toast with onion marmalade, 18
tofu, in kushikatsu, 17
tomato/es
  cherry, in picnic vegetable salad, 76–7
  cherry, in small stuffed vegetables, 49, 52
  cherry, in tournedoes de saumon, 96
  dried, 57
  in ragout of baby vegetables, 52–3
  red pepper sauce, 30
  sauce
    raw, 52
    raw yellow, 52
  in vegetables à la Grecque, 52
  vine-ripened, stuffed with sugar snap peas, 48
Tommy's roll, 13, 16–17
Tommy Tang's Siamese Café, 13
tonkatsu sauce, 16
torte, broccoli, 45–6
tortelli, black and white on-a-stick, 29–30, 32
tortillas, blue corn, with smoked salmon and
    American caviar, 28
tournedos de saumon, 96
Tower, Jeremiah, 9, 117, 123
Trader Vic, 8
Trefethen, Janet, 68, 132, 145, 152
Trefethen, Katie, 156
Trefethen Vineyards, 68, 132, 145, 152, 156
truffle(s)
  juice in madeira sauce, 121
  in the leopard's dish, 85, 87
  sauce, 18
  with warm vegetable salad, 64–5
Trumps, 8, 72, 73, 125
Trumps Cuban sandwich, 125
tuma cheese, in mixed cheese filling for pizza
    rustica, 88
tuna (fresh)
  in ahi carpaccio, 18
  salad, grilled, 100–01
  with tangerine butter sauce, 101
turkey, in avocado chef salad, 77
turnips
  baby, in pigeon with chanterelles and baby

California vegetables, 124–5
baby, in summer vegetable plate, 61
baked with cream, 121
Tutto Italia, 45, 81, 137

U do's almond tile cookies, 152

V alentino, 8, 133
vanilla soufflé, 161
veal
fillet with green peppercorn sauce, 133
ground, in ragout for the leopard's dish, 87
loin, roast, with shallots and wild mushroom
sauce, 132–3
osso buco, 133–4
piccata, 133
vitello marinato Parmigiano e olio di tartufo,
18
vegetable(s)
à la Grecque, 52
baby California, and pigeon with
chanterelles, 124–5
baby, ragout, 52–3
chili, 53
grilled, 117
salad, picnic, 76–7
salad, warm, with truffles, 64–5
small, stuffed with shrimp ratatouille and two
sauces, 49, 52
summer plate, 61
summer, with quails, 121
see also under individual names
Velvet Turtle, 36
Venezia, Joe, 9, 101, 106
Venice Beach seafood soup, 40–41
Vincenti, Mauro, 8
vinaigrette
for artichokes, 45
dressing, 92
for green beans with scallop eggs, 69
for picnic vegetable salad, 77
raspberry, 96
tarragon, 65
see also under dressing
vitello marinato Parmigiano e olio di tartufo, 18

wagon wheel pasta salad, 92
walnut
bread, 156
pasta salad, 92
watercress, wild, dressing with lobster, 106
Waters, Alice, 9, 12, 61, 80, 84
white mousse cake with zest of grapefruit and
pine nuts, 153

Y amaguchi, Roy, 9, 21, 71, 73
yogurt gazpacho, cold, 43
Yoriki, 16

Z ucchini
baby, in pigeon with chanterelles and baby
California vegetables, 124–5
baby, in quails with summer vegetables, 121
baby, in ragout of vegetables, 52
boats, 61
bread, 161
and chicken, stir-fried, 128
in vegetables à la Grecque, 52
zucchini flowers
in small stuffed vegetables with shrimp
ratatouille and two sauces, 49, 52
stuffed, 49

NOTES